Maurice Harris

Selected addresses

Maurice Harris

Selected addresses

ISBN/EAN: 9783337276980

Printed in Europe, USA, Canada, Australia, Japan

Cover: Foto ©Andreas Hilbeck / pixelio.de

More available books at **www.hansebooks.com**

SELECTED ADDRESSES

BY

MAURICE H. HARRIS, Ph.D.,

MINISTER TEMPLE ISRAEL OF HARLEM

NEW YORK

SECOND SERIES

NEW YORK

PHILIP COWEN, 213–215 EAST 44TH STREET

1895

CONTENTS.

SHYLOCK.

Among the many forms of persecution of the Jews, that of misrepresenting him in fiction is not the mildest. From the legend of the "Wandering Jew," who eternally suffers for his brutality to Jesus of Nazareth, down to the Fagin of Charles Dickens—or, to be very up-to-date, shall we add Du Maurier's "Svengali?"—the world has always been regaled with some revolting specimen of humanity depicted as a typical Jew. And this form of persecution is the most lasting. Surely the effect of Hadrian's cruelty to the Jews of the Roman Empire was dissipated ages ago, but Chaucer's vilification in the "Canterbury Tales" will continue its influence as long as his poetry is read. One of the most notorious types created by fiction that has helped the world to misunderstand us in some respects, and yet the better understand us in others, is that of Shylock. Its importance is largely due to the genius of its creator, Shakespeare.

We find two distinct opinions about this character. When the world thought the Jew a monster, the character of Shylock was so depicted; since public opinion of the Jew has changed, it has correspondingly modified its interpretation, maintaining that it was intended as a vindication instead of a vilification. Perhaps there is reason for both of these impressions even to-day. We seem to detect two distinct currents in its delineation. On the one hand, we find Shylock fulfilling the popular opinion and satisfying the popular prejudice—a bloodthirsty miser, without conscience and without pity. On the other hand, we detect Shakespeare's protest against the cruel treatment of a class of human beings too little understood, and then Shylock appears to us as a long-suffering creature, to whom the world refuses the commonest justice or consideration. Many would have liked this latter impression to have been so pronounced that there would be no doubt about it. This would have defeated the very purpose intended, apart from the fact that it would offend the canons of art to permit the moral to appear too plainly. Unless the picture of the Jew, Shylock was to represent, did in some way satisfy the prejudiced expectations, the character would have been hissed off the stage, and Shakespeare might either have been sent to "The Tower" or stoned to death by the savage mob of the Elizabethan age.

We must understand the condition of the times. Although the glorious reign of "good Queen Bess" and the Augustan age of English literature, it was still the rough civilization of the Middle Ages, when it needed little provocation to draw sword, and when barbaric cruelty was revealed even in punishments of the law—for mutilation was a common penalty. It was but in the preceding reign that heretics were burned at slow fires in the market-place of Smithfield, to the great delectation of the populace.

The world of the sixteenth century still knew little of the Jew, nor did it try to understand him. In the popular imagination, the Jews were a race accursed of God, who had crucified humanity's Saviour—society's outcasts, whom it was a virtue to abuse. Some of the peasantry even believed that a Jew was a four-footed animal ! This ignorance had, furthermore, a better excuse in England than elsewhere, where the Jew had been nominally expelled since 1290, three hundred years before, though we now know that a few scattered Jews were in England even during the years of their presumed exile. The physician Lopez, put to death at Tyburn on the charge of poisoning. which was never satisfactorily proven, may have come in contact with Shakespeare, and some claim he was the model for Shylock.

If, then, we are not quite satisfied with the character of Shylock, if it does not come up to our expectation of a vindication of a much-abused people, yet when we compare it with the popular representation, we can better understand what we owe to Shakespeare for attempting to give to the character of the Jew at least some human traits. The "Jew of Malta" (Barabas), by Marlowe, a contemporary of Shakespeare, is a monster to whom no evil deed is foreign, and who commits his outrages by wholesale. Gosson's "Jew" is equally repulsive; and yet these creatures who committed all crimes known to the time, seemed to please the theatrical audiences of the Elizabethan age, and to be accepted as fair representations of Jews. Shylock had his faults, but Shylock is at least a man. Furthermore, the incidents of the story of the "Merchant of Venice" were not created by Shakespeare, for you are aware that he hardly invented the plot of a single one of his plays. He simply used materials already at hand, giving, with the marvelous touch of his genius, immortality to legends that otherwise would have passed into oblivion, and making the characters of folk-lore stand forth as living beings, models for all ages. Even the combining of two old stories in this play before us, the story of the bond, the pound of flesh, and the story of the three caskets, had already been done by previous authors. Even the incident of a woman impersonating a lawyer had been introduced in a previous rendering of this story.

Since Shakespeare had few types around him from which to judge the real character of the Jew, and only the distortions of prejudice in the fictitious representations, he had largely to fall back upon the Bible for suggestions of Jewish character. His free use of Scripture in this play is seen by frequent quotation. Shylock appeals to "Father Abraham," swears by "Jacob's staff," calls his servant a "fool of Hagai's offspring," and Portia "a Daniel come to judgment." "My deeds upon my head," he says again. He compares his means of increasing his wealth to the way that Jacob multiplied the flocks he earned from Laban, calling forth the derisive comment, "The devil cites Scripture."

It is unfortunate that he should select Jacob the crafty rather than Samuel the seer, Isaiah the preacher of righteousness, or Moses the liberator, as a prevailing type from which to draw his illustrations. He was again limited to the expectations of his time. The world was not yet ready for "Nathan der Weise." He may also have had in mind the Jew as depicted in the New Testament, popularly supposed to have crucified the Savior, and usually characterized as a worshiper of the letter of the law and the ignorer of the spirit—the pseudo-Pharisee. Still Shylock is a man more sinned against than sinning, whom the inhumanity of the whole world has made inhuman. Long brooding over the shameful treatment of his people has marred his character and life and dried up the founts of tenderness in his bosom; yet Shylock is a scholar, a man of more general knowledge than any of the other characters in the play.

I will not attempt to tell the story, and will only bring forward those portions in which Shylock is represented. Shylock is a money-lender—of course! And the outside world seeks him only when it wishes to borrow money—of course! This is the stereotyped setting of the Jew, which all the third-rate melodramatists have since followed.

In Shylock's reply te Antonio's request for the loan, Shakespeare at once skilfully brings before us the popular treatment of the Jew:

> Many a time and oft
> In the Rialto you have rated me
> About my moneys and my usuances.
> Still have I borne it with a patient shrug,
> For sufferance is the badge of all our tribe
> You call me misbeliever, cut-throat dog.
> And spit on my Jewish gaberdine,
> And all for use of that which is mine own.
> You, that did void your rheum upon my beard.
> And foot me as you spurn a stranger cur
> Over your threshold.

Shakespeare is telling us how the Jew of his day was treated—how he may even have seen him treated in foreign lands.

Not only Shylock is protesting against this treatment, but Shakespeare also. When he makes such coarse and savage handling come from the hero of the story, who is otherwise an ideal character, a gentleman, one of nature's noblemen, the injustice of the world to the Jew is the more distinctly brought out. He shows us that an individual, otherwise irreproachable, has inherited a habitual contempt for the Jew, in which he indulges as second nature.

Shylock hates Antonio, because Antonio "hates his sacred nation." He represents all that is antagonistic in the Christian, and Shylock feels that there are concentrated in Antonio the enmities that have been the cause of all the woes of his race for generations. And yet, in this recital of his wrongs to the man who comes to borrow money, we detect a hidden appeal—an appeal for better treatment, for but a lull in the monotony of his contumely. For he asks again :

> " Is it possible
> A cur can lend three thousand ducats? Or,
> Shall I bend low, and in a bondman's key,

> With bated b'eath and whispering humbleness
> Say this :
> ' Fair sir, you spat on me on Wednesday last;
> You spurned me such a day; another time
> You called me dog; and for these courtesies
> I'll lend you thus much moneys?' "

But Antonio, characterized as a man so full of compassion for every creature—but the Jew, is deaf to this appeal, and heartlessly replies:

> " I am as like to call thee so again,
> To spit on thee again, to spurn thee too."

In desperation, Shylock determines on a strange move. He will loan the money to the enemy, to the man that reviles him and his race; to the man that represents in himself all that is inimical to the Jew and all that has embittered the Jewish life. He will loan the money; if it be returned in time he will take no interest; he will pour coals of fire upon his head, and teach him who holds as doctrine—the loving of the enemy, a something of the practice of it. But if the money be not returned in time, then he will exact from him such a bond that he will have his life at his mercy, and see whether Antonio will not change his contemptuous tone, and humble himself before the despised Jew.

I do not think that, at this stage of the story, Shylock really contemplates taking the life of his enemy; but events are hurrying on. His daughter deserts him—the only family tie left—robs him of his money, and renounces his faith. And these very acts that in ordinary life would earn her the world's condemnation, performed against a Jew, win her the world's approval. All praise Jessica; none reproach her. Her unnatural conduct, her deception of her father, her heartless abandonment and exploitation of him, her joining the camp of his enemies—directed against a Jew, become her merits and the hope of her future salvation. Shylock then finds himself deserted and robbed by the one in all the world who should stand by him. He sees the people gathering around him and jeering at him; none have sympathy for his trouble. No; he is a Jew. They take a fiendish joy in the added calamities, that now come pouring thick upon him. Tubal brings the news that his daughter has sold her dead mother's ring, given to her father when he was a bachelor. Another says, he knows the tailor who made the wings with which she flew away. Another reminds him that he is no more like his daughter than jet like ivery. Antonio himself, his arch-enemy, assists in the girl's escape. One calls him "old carrion;" another, "devil likeness of a Jew;" while faithless Jew," foul Jew," and "dog-Jew" are common epithets by which he is addressed.

And now, at the very acme of his despair, he learns that his enemy, Antonio, cannot repay his debt, and his life is at his mercy. Standing at bay, stung by the reproaches and gibes of all around him, outraged by the heartlessness of their cruelty, not one to take his side, rejected and outcast by the whole world, he makes a desperate resolve to have, at least, revenge upon one of his tormentors. In the tragic dignity in which he rehearses the wrongs of himself and his people, Shylock rises to his highest. A feeling of awe, perhaps of shame, steals over his auditors as he reminds them that a Jew is a human being, and none can answer him.

"He hath disgraced me and hindered me half a million; laughed at my losses, mocked at my gains, scorned my nation, thwarted my bargains, cooled my friends, heated mine enemies; and what's his reason? I am a Jew. Hath not a Jew eyes? Hath not a Jew hands, organs, dimensions, senses, affections, passions? Fed with the same food, hurt with the same weapons, subject to the same diseases, healed by the same means, warmed and cooled by the same winter and summer as a Christian is? If you prick us, do we not bleed? If you poison us, do we not die? And if you wrong us, shall we not revenge? If we are like you in the rest, we will resemble you in that. If a Jew wrong a Christian, what is his humility? Revenge. If a Christian wrong a Jew, what should his sufferance be by Christian example? Why, revenge. The villainy you teach me I will execute, and it shall go hard, but I will better the instruction."

This is the wail of the Jew through centuries; this is the cry that went up from Egypt, from the Roman amphitheatre, from the dungeons of the Inquisition. We hear its echo all through the Dark Ages; and the genius of Shakespeare voices it as it had never been voiced before or since. The tables are turned; he has his enemy "on the hip," and those who spurned him once are appealing to him now and begging him to forgive the bond—that is, all except Antonio, the man most concerned.

A magnificent appeal is made to his mercy, but it cannot wipe out the wrongs of ages that have entered into his very nature, embittered his whole being. He cannot in a moment forget the inhuman treatment that has been meted out to him from day to day. There stands his enemy, and even now will not recall one jot of the brutal treatment which he had daily dealt him.

To the very last Antonio accuses him of every evil and denies him every virtue; he will die sooner than be humble or even respectful to a Jew.

> " I pray you, think you question with a Jew:
> You may as well go stand upon the beach
> And bid the main flood bate its usual height;
> You may as well forbid the mountain pines
> To wag their high tops and to make no noise,
> When they are fretten with the gusts of heaven;
> · You may as well do anything most hard,
> As seek to soften that—than which what's harder?—
> His Jewish heart."

Shylock may have waited for a word of kindness, a petition for clemency from this one man, that would bid him pause in the execution of his bond. Antonio is doggedly silent and Shylock is doggedly determined.

We know the upshot of the trial at its opening scene. We know that the fair words used to the Jew, that he must certainly have justice, are mere pretence, that they are but the reasoning of the wolf with the lamb he is about to swallow. Portia's final rejection of Shylock's suit is all prepared, even while at first she seems to give it temporary defence. Even when making that famous appeal to his mercy, she is only playing with him—she will not need it. Shylock does not receive the bond—do we not know it beforehand?—does not even receive the money loaned—we had anticipated that, too. Half of his fortune must be given to the faithless daughter who has renounced him and to the man who stole her from him, and he is told that he is under obligation to the hated Antonio for the retention of the other half, and that he may feel very thankful that he escapes with his life. Furthermore, he must forego his religion and become a Christian.

The treatment here received was the treatment meted out to the Jew in every clime and under every condition. The conflict of Jew with Christian is a conflict of the weak against the strong, with one monotonous result. They ask Shylock for mercy ; they refuse to grant him justice. And although he does not appear more upon the scene, we can follow his career to the end—saddened by misfortune when sitting in his lonely home, and when he ventures forth, there is no doubt that Antonio again spits on his gaberdine with added malice, and the crowd now more than ever jeers him, calls him dog and mocks at his reverses.

Shakespeare has attempted to plead the cause of the

Jew and eloquently to set forth his wrongs, and also to give a touch of the human to a type hitherto represented as monstrous. That his is not the true type of the Jew either, goes without saying. It is hardly necessary to defend ourselves against it. Perhaps the falsest incident in the play is Shylock's boldness before the law. Dare a Jew, whom all could revile and abuse without restraint or hope of redress for him, insistently demand the exact letter of justice in the public courts, in the presence of the duke, and threaten the city of Venice with the loss of its charter? If the law permitted him to resent his wrongs in that way, the very occasion for the trial would never have arisen, and the "Merchant of Venice" could not have been written.

Though Shakespeare may have charitably supposed that the harsh and unfair treatment meted to the Jew was largely responsible for so unlovable and unlovely a creature as Shylock, and has attempted to convey this in the play, we need hardly say that even such treatment failed to produce a Shylock. The Jew of the Middle Ages may have been dreadfully demoralized by bad treatment, but Shylock was not his photograph. Shakespeare has certainly no intimate acquaintance with Jewish characteristics; his representations are borrowed from popular rumor.

While justified in seeking revenge, the Jew has been the last to demand it. If there is a distinct failing in him it is that he has forgiven his enemies too easily; he has too readily forgotten the wrongs of the past. The picture of the Jew sharpening his knife on his shoe, baring the breast of his enemy and ready to stab him to the heart, is so antagonistic to his character that it need not even be defended. And renouncing his faith, too, without a protest—so like a Jew!

Shylock is a miser. His first words when introduced

upon the stage are, "Three thousand ducats." When he dreams, he dreams of "money-bags." When his daughter has fled with the jewels, he says: "Would that my daughter were dead at my feet and the jewels in her ears." He bewails his money first and his daughter second. His servant complains that he is starved. Shakespeare here but records that popular delusion of the extravagant love of money by the Jew, that was simply a misconstruction of the fact that the restrictions of law confined the Jew to money-trading, and not only shut him out from every other walk of life, from the professions and public career, but excluded him from honorable and cultured society, from the refining and relaxing enjoyments of life, when he might have outlet for *the spending of his money.*

But when Jessica says, "Our house is hell," and seems to feel so little hesitation in leaving her father and so little affection for him, we think that here is a side of Jewish life that never was presented to Shakespeare—the domestic. Ties of affection, binding closely together all the inmates of the Jewish home, is one of the character-istics of the race, that has been recognized and reluctantly acknowledged even by his enemies. Finally, the contrast between the two religions is all that we may expect. What is noble is Christian, and what is contemptible is Jewish. The Christian has a disinterested love for his fellow-man, the Jew worships the letter of the law as his ideal.

"The Hebrew will turn Christian," says Antonio; "he grows kind." This injustice to our faith, the misunder-standing of our character, is dying out as the world is learning to know us better; and yet it still exists. Com-parisons between the two creeds of the character found in this play, but a little more veiled, are still voiced in the literature of the nineteenth century; and with all the world's tardy recognition of some of its mistakes against us, we have still abundant reason to say with Shylock : " Suffrance is the badge of all our tribe."

A PASSING WORD ABOUT OUR COUNTRY.

It is not easy to judge one's own country. We are
not able to stand off from it and look at it objectively,
although occasionally, from the criticisms of foreigners,
we are enabled " to see ourselves as others see us." Let
us first try to consider the political situation in relation
to the commercial, 'and immediately the difficulties of
judging our own present themselves. When the two
great parties moralize about the political outlook, it is
customary for each to ascribe all great calamities to the
administration of its opponent, and all prosperity to
itself. From such expressions of prejudice at least we
will try to be free; we will leave them for the demagogue
on the eve of election; but meeting here as non-partisan
as biased mortals can be, with no political contest
before us to confuse our judgment, let us try to look
beyond the narrow orbit of party limitations and take a
larger, fairer view, judging things as they are and letting
facts tell their own tale.

I.

The affairs of a nation, its commercial and interna-
tional relations are so complex that it is hard to decide,
if we would decide exactly, what may be the direct cause
or causes of prosperity and of adversity. For the
moment we talk about causes and consequence, we enter
upon speculative ground. We can but presume, and 'if
we would approach the truth, we must take many varying
data into consideration. We must not confuse causes of
events with the immediate occasion that brings them
about. The tax on tea was the occasion that led to the

Declaration of Independence; but the cause was, perhaps, that the colonists had reached political manhood—they were able to govern themselves. Nor may we presume that that which follows is that which results. Night follows day, but does not result from it. The country may be prosperous during a certain administration, and its prosperity may be owing to the administration that preceded it; or the adversity of a nation may be due to a policy that is about to be introduced, and whose effect is felt even in anticipation. Says the Democrat: The panic of '93 was due to McKinleyism that preceded it. Says the Republican: It was due to the expectation of low tariff. Sometimes even superabundance may defeat the very prosperity it is supposed to imply, as the over-production of cotton, some two years back, made the supply greater than the demand, lowered the price and spoilt the trade of the producer. We have instances of dairymen who had deliberately spilt part of their milk in order to keep up the price, finding that they could get larger profits in that way, and of grain-growers who had burned quantities of wheat for the same reason. Some economic philosophers will even ascribe panics to spots on the sun, which is surely out of the reach of both Republicans and Democrats!

Personally, I do not think that " protection," so-called, or tariff reduction, caused the depression in the commerce of last year. If we can trace the origin at all—and we can never be sure of that—it may, perhaps, have been caused by over-production, by a haste to be rich, by dangerous speculation. I think that if the tendency of the time is toward prosperity, no party, however mistaken its theories, can ever absolutely prevent it. If a particular depression is to arise, it will come in spite of the political doctrine and political practice of the party of the majority. While it may affect the individual here and there, to the public at large it matters little what the tariff may be, provided the people are satisfied it is not going to be interfered with. Oliver Wendell Holmes well said, that if all the medicine were poured into the sea, the public health would very much improve. And so I think if Congress, or particularly the Senate, would take a vacation for ten years, we would all enjoy the benefit of the change, as the man who gave his wife a holiday for the benefit of his health.

Without wishing to take either side, I would favor the policy whose tendency is towards ultimate free trade, simply because it is that side that implies a minimum of interference of the government in the affairs of the people. We approach the idea of a commonwealth when government is reduced to its lowest terms, and does nothing that can be done as well by the individual, and intrudes its legislation and restriction into no institution or interest of the people that can be as wisely and as safely managed without its aid. This takes us back to the first principles of government. Leave the trade of the country alone, it will take care of itself ; it will adjust itself to its own advantages and deficiencies. We can never know what harm we can do by our artificial bolstering and equalization and bounty-giving. Even the so-called fostering of infant industries demands a mastery of all the niceties of political economy, or the government will make a mess of things it does not quite understand. And it seems to me that some of those " infant industries " have been at the breast of the nation after they had already reached vigorous youth, able to tussle around with their equals and shift for themselves.

As we are gradually modifying our original Constitution in the light of a later wisdom and a larger experience, I think the tendency will be to discourage a too frequent change in the political complexion of the country, and thereby to keep it and its trade in a more stable condition. We are all prepared for an enactment that will lengthen the term of the President, and make a second term unconstitutional. In this way people will be able to adjust their business affairs on the advent of a new administration to a larger limit of time, knowing that they will not be disturbed. Stability is one of the qualities we Americans have yet to acquire, both in our doings and in our characters.

We hope gradually, on the theory just stated,—that that government is ideal that interferes to the least extent,— gradually to withdraw from politics many subordinate positions in the public service which are not affected by the policy of the national parties; for instance, the large number of positions in the Post Office and Police departments, and that gradually civil service reform will take the place of that barbaric doctrine, "To the victor belongs the spoils."

Perhaps the most important victory won by our State on the 6th of November was the victory least talked about—the separation for all future elections of municipal and national affairs. Henceforward, our city needs will not be complicated by national issues, nor will we have to sacrifice the introduction of desirable improve- ments, or the removal of undesirable abuses, in order to elect the Governor of our party, or to uphold our national policy.

———

II.

While each State is right in jealously guarding its autonomy and its freedom; at the same time, the hour is ripe for a closer welding of the American people as a whole. It is well that we should coalesce into a more compact community, and feel that we are not a federation of provinces, jealous of each other's privileges, but that the State boundaries are lost in the larger line that surrounds the nationality, that links us as a great nation —the great American people. Let us entrust more power with the central head of our government. When an emergency comes, let him not feel that his hands are tied, and that if he does take vigorous action, as the President did in the railroad strike in Chicago last July, he need not be criticized by State Governors, who question his authority and regarded his action as an infringement on their State privileges.

I read some time ago, in a European survey of American institutions, that a particular organization, in drawing up its constitution, hesitated to speak of the American *nation*, fearing that the word might be objected to, deftly substituting for it "people of the United States." Why should we be afraid of the use of the word "nation?" Why should we fear being welded firmly into a great nationality? Nationality in the past has been the inspiration for great achievement in all high and noble directions, in religion, in art, in civilization. Israel commenced its upward growth under the rule of Samuel, when it began to feel conscious of the fact that it was not any longer a federation of tribes. With the sense of nationality came patriotism, and the patriotism deepened into a larger moral sense that reached to every son of Israel. Never did the German people rise to their true dignity until their States were moulded into an Empire.

It is true that America has become the great haven for all the refugees and misfits of the world, since people from wholly civilized and semi-civilized nations alike, hie hither, hoping to find here a fairer field, with no favor or prejudice, no class legislation, a larger opportunity for carrying on the struggle for existence. This constant influx of foreigners, whose arrival is not yet over, delays the homogeneity of the American people. It must also not be forgotten that this country, which is virtually a continent. represents many stages of civilization Seeing, as we do, the high degree of cultivation, the complete reign of law and order, and the beautifully laid out and densely-populated cities of a few chosen Eastern States, that enjoy, perhaps, the world's best product in all directions, we are likely to forget that there are large tracts of land which even the pioneer has barely trodden, rude settlements of rough-and-ready life, of which Bret Harte's descriptions are still hardly exaggerations. These conditions explain, if they do not excuse, the wild brigandage and lawlessness of which our newspapers furnish such lurid accounts. The frequent homicide of the South shows that the baneful influences of slavery that have survived its abolition are not yet extinct; while the centres of Negro, Indian and Chinese life that we can never expect to assimilate with our Caucasian nationality, all tend to complicate our national problem.

III.

For all of these reasons we do not find patriotism as deep-seated in the people as a whole as we would wish, although it is very intense with some. The cosmopolitan is abroad ; half the people we meet have roots in other lands. In pointing to lack of patriotism, I need hardly say I do not mean that vulgar braggadocio that boasts of superiority, but that love of country that is willing to sacrifice local pride, partisan prejudice, and sectarian or foreign sentiment for the attainment of its nation's highest ideals. The national parties do not always select their noblest men for the highest offices of State. It is proverbial that our best citizens have rarely been Presidents. The party leaders know that State prejudice is stronger than national patriotism, than many are likely to vote for an indifferent man from their own State rather than for a much greater man from some other State. And they pander to these prejudices and foster them. They do not love their heroes for the enemies they make, but defeat them or pass them over for the very reasons that should have recommended them to the highest confidences of the people. They prefer a "safe" candidate to an ideal official. They do not encourage hero-worship but give the crown of glory to the average man thus stamping mediocrity with their highest approval.

I was exceedingly disappointed when even the Committee of Seventy, that body of eminent men, when presenting their candidates for the offices of this city, at a critical moment when a great moral lesson was to be taught to the people and they were exhorted that party fealty must be sacrificed for municipal purity, that even at such a moment they stooped to pander to the prejudices of foreign nationalities, thus robbing their victory of a something of its moral force. They must needs have a German candidate to win over the German element and an Irish candidate to satisfy the Irish element. Now, a regard felt for the land which was our first home, in which we first drew breath, even long after we have officially renounced our allegiance to it has its root in a good and worthy sentiment which I would not for the world discourage, since its absence is a something

baser than ingratitude and more unnatural than filial
disrespect.

> "Lives there a man with soul so dead
> That never to himself has said,
> This is my own, my native land."

But when our regard felt for an individual coming
from the same place across the waters, is going to
interfere with our duties to the nation of our adoption,
when we dare to confuse its interests with that sentiment,
we are no longer patriots, but betrayers.

IV.

Perhaps the greatest lesson that America has taught
the world is the lesson of equality, not that "all men are
equal,"—that sophistry has long since been given up.
The truth lies in its negative side, in not recognizing
artificial superiority; in judging men not by their ante-
cedents, but by themselves. But even here a warning
must be uttered. We must be all the more ready to
recognize real superiority and not be jealous of
excellence, because it emphasizes the inequality between
man and man. It must not teach us to be too satisfied
with the average man, or to feel that one man is as good
as another, since that depends upon whom the other
happens to be. It is a principle properly understood
that it is an inspiration to the artisan, and will certainly
teach the humblest individual the true dignity of manhood. It is one of the secrets of our coming greatness.
A few parvenus are beginning to be ashamed of it.
Honi soit qui mal y pense.

In comparison with any of the nations of Europe, we
have many advantages. We stand aloof and alone, too

far to be embroiled in the great wars growing out of
petty jealousies of bordering monarchs, untroubled by
the vexed question of the balance of power, indifferent
as to whether France take a slice more or a slice less of
Siam, whether Russia may reach the Mediterranean, or
England get control of Central Africa. It is also exceedingly advantageous that, large as the country is, it is
compact ; it holds all its parts together in one closely
joined whole from Alaska to Texas. It has not to keep
battalions and fleets at distant points of the globe to
guard remote colonies. It is very glad that it has not
the boast of Great Britain that "the sun never sets upon
its possessions." And so, desiring no territorial enlarge-
ment and fearing no territorial curtailment, not needing
to maintain vast armies in order to preserve peace,
which is the paradox presented to us by the great
nations of Europe, it is able to give itself up to the
peaceful arts of industry and to the development of its
own resources. If it enters foreign politics at all, it is
usually on humanitarian grounds, as, for instance, in its
present attempt to hasten peace between China and
Japan.

VI.

We must not suppose, as of course we do not, that all our
problems are worked out, or that our work is done. Our
greatest achievements still lie before us. Emerson has
said that "America is another name for opportunity."
We are a young nation; we have all the enthusiasm and
impetuosity of the young, their virtues and their failings;
we are in a great hurry to accomplish all things; we are
ever seeking new worlds to conquer; we are still too
intense, and, as some one has put it, "personal life is

'developed at the expense of race life." We have not yet
won the repose and the dignity of maturity. Let us
understand that we have no need to apologize for not
having achieved greatness in the higher walks of life, or
for not having given many geniuses of literature to the
world, or for not having founded schools in art; nor need
we be so eager to resent these lacks in our development,
when pointed out by others. In subduing a continent
and preparing it for our use, in organizing it as a great
commonwealth, in making it the home of vast industries,
in winning renown for excellence of mechanism, in
solving many social problems, and in giving a new
chance to the "submerged tenth," we have surely done
our share towards the cause of civilization. The rest will
come, and it will come all the better of itself, if we do
not try to force it by artificial urging. When we have completely mastered and finished the material, the intellectual
and that which is something more than intellectual—
that we call culture—will win its own place. All perfect
growth must be slow growth. We cannot expect to build
up a literary centre as they build up a city in the West,
unless we wish our literary centre to be as ephemeral as
the Western town. Haste has always been the enemy of
depth and thoroughness. In the American it is largely
due to a wonderful industry. For he has taught the
world the dignity of labor, so that idleness is no longer
esteemed. But, as Mr. Herbert Spencer said to us, we
have preached the gospel of work long enough; it is time
we begin preaching the gospel of relaxation. When we
have learned to work a little more slowly, a little more
thoroughly, when we have learned to prize quality more
than quantity, and realized the priceless value of leisure,
and the refinement and the aspiration towards higher
things, for which it gives us the opportunity in our lives,
a new era of our nation will have begun.

VII.

And a word about the American Jew. Like many of the persecuted people from other lands, from the days of the Puritans, who sought these shores that they might have a place to rest their head, where they could honestly worship God as their hearts dictated, the Jewish people feel cause for gratitude that Providence guided the pioneers of this nation in the liberal and free principles on which they decided to base it. We Jews have brought a record of loyalty and patriotism to every land that has permitted us to make it a home. We have not forgotten it here. We should, therefore, resent the distinction between Jew and American, that is sometimes made "American," in that sense signifying Gentile. The inference is an insult, and implies that the Jew is less of an American than the Gentile, that he is a something of an alien, a denizen rather than a citizen.

Let us be proud of the title of American, let us always claim it, and let us never permit the use of it as discriminating against us. Jews are not the only emigrants to these shores. There are many German Gentiles who have come here within the last ten years, while there were many American Jews in the War of the Revolution. We are as American as Mr. Schurz or Mr. Erhardt, the Germans; as Mr. Gilroy or Mr. Goff, the Irishmen ; as the late President McCosh or Mr. Carnegie, the Scotchmen ; as Professor Chandler or Dr. Collyer, the Englishmen.

But we cannot be too cautious in the wise use of the perfect liberty and equality that is given us with the people among whom we live. There was a reserve in the Jew of half a century back, partly but not entirely due to social ostracism and to the religious differences between him and his neighbor ; and yet, even under the present circumstances, it might be well to retain a something of that reserve in a somewhat different and higher sense. Let us not hasten to claim the very limit of our civil and social prerogatives ; nor need we push to the front to put ourselves in evidence because we are no longer mobbed with the cry of " Hep ! Hep !" behind us when we appear in public. Let us cultivate our pride, and not be in too much of a hurry to rush into the arms of those who are not yet ready to give us their full and unqualified esteem. We must be jealous of our honor, and accept perfect social equality, or none. It is lowering to our dignity to be admitted on a plane of compromise, as lower dependents at ancient tables sat "below the salt."

But let us earn a higher place by showing a more active participance in all reformative and patriotic movements of our country. Let us record ourselves ever on the better side, the side of right, of purity, of reformation. Ah ! if we could win in America a something of the reputation that was enjoyed by our ancestors in Spain—holding places in the high councils of the nation, enjoying its confidence, guiding its affairs, its golden age and ours !

RELIGIOUS ENTHUSIASM.

As we read the old story again, and the Maccabean picture is once more before us, we see the patriots tearing down the mountain fastnesses to charge upon the ranks of their Syrian opponents. We are not surprised to learn that though their numbers were so small and their enemies so great, yet, in skirmish after skirmish, they routed them. We see them inspired with a great resolve, enkindled with religious fervor, and we realize that this intensity of purpose more than made up for deficiency of numbers. With the battle-cry, "Who is like unto Thee among the mighty?" written on their standard, they entered the field, and, with that sentiment glowing in their hearts, who could withstand the band of religious patriots as they bore down upon their enemies, carried along with a torrent of impetuous enthusiasm?

Enthusiasm makes difficulties easy, if it does not even deny their existence. If we were to go back to the root of the word, we would find that it means " possessed of God," recalling the old belief that the divinity entered into the body of the individual that it would move, making it a passive agent of its purposes. The old words live, though the old beliefs have died, or rather, they have become modified into metaphors. Enthusiasm still has for us almost all of its original sense, and, with almost literal exactness, we still feel that the man enthused is the man God-possessed. The divinity is upon him and within him, it is spurring him and impelling him, raising him above his ordinary self and his ordinary capacities. The athlete steps back many paces in order to give himself the proper purchase for a great leap, and rushes down to the starting-point, reaches it

when the acme of his ability is attained and the
momentum raised to its highest point, and is enabled to
exhibit the perfection of his powers. The man enthusiastic is the human strung to a divine pitch. He, too,
feels the swell and surge of his great purpose, impelling
and urging him on; and as the idea, if it be an idea, or
the action, if it be an action, grows in grandeur and
hopefulness, in his glowing imagination, at last, borne
on by the torrent of his fervor, he springs upon his final
purpose, hardly seeing the obstacles that shatter to pieces
before the impetuosity of his ardor; and accomplishment
seems easy, natural, inevitable. So genius is rarely discouraged; for often the magnitude of the difficulty
kindles a corresponding enthusiasm that comes with
yet greater force by the impetus of resistance.

Enthusiasm is in action what speed is in motion.
Putting it mathematically, the power of the force would
be proportioned to its velocity, and so in action, the
power of our attainment is proportioned to the impetuosity. Just as we will often overcome an obstacle in our
path by quick motion, so the ardor of enthusiasm that
bursts from the soul breaks down the impediment in the
path that a lesser force of slower motion would not overcome. "There are no Alps," said Napoleon, when he
learns that they are to bar his progress. "Impossible is
a word known only in the dictionary of fools." There
were no Alps to Napoleon; his enthusiasm levelled them;
the force of his tremendous will made his purpose iron,
and the Alps melted away like the snows on top of them.
"I will be marshal of France," said a Frenchman; and
if we had heard the enthusiasm of the tone, we would
not have been surprised that the ambition was attained.
You can be marshal of France or marshal of the world,
if you are prepared to say it with the same confident
intensity.

What is the difference between enthusiasm and zeal? Permit me to create a synonym that may not always be borne out in practice. Enthusiasm is joyous; zeal is severe There is a glad ring in the voice of the man of enthusiasm; there is at times a wail of sadness, and in its extreme form, even a harsh, grating note in the voice of zeal. The prophets are oftener zealous than they are enthusiastic. In that respect they differ from the psalmists. They speak largely of the awful and terrible day of the Lord; they see the wickedness of man and its awful consequences; they predict the righteous wrath of a righteous God visiting the sins of backsliding man. Turn to the Psalms. How different is the tone, at least as a whole. " My soul thirsteth for God, for the living God." " Lift up your heads, oh ye gates, and be ye uplifted, ye everlasting doors, and the King of glory shall come in. Who is the King of glory? The Lord strong and mighty, He is the King of glory." " Exult, oh ye righteous, in the Lord." " Let the cedars of Lebanon shout for joy." " Praise ye the Lord from the heavens, praise him in the heights. Kings, people, princes, judges, young men, maidens, old men, children, let them praise the name of the Lord, let everything that has breath praise the Lord."

We see the exact contrast of enthusiasm and zeal in the character of Hillel and Shammai. Shammai, the stern and passionate, bids the mocking heathen begone. Hillel, the serene, in whom cheer bubbles forth as a perennial spring, takes the scoffer by the hand and makes him a worshiper. Ezra, the zealous, summons Israel as to the judgment seat, and tells them of the awful consequences of the disobedience of the law, and imposes upon them an injunction that fills them with sadness and woe. Nehemiah, the enthusiastic, looks at the hopeful side; seeing the ruined temple, he gathers brave men about him and builds up the walls. " I have been zealous for the Lord of Hosts," says Elijah despondently.' " Yes," reply the Rabbins, " too zealous, and, therefore, was the brook of Cherith dried up, and he was made to suffer thirst, because his zeal, untouched with clemency, led him to cruel extremes, when he declared a three years' drought on the land for its sins.

The earnestness of the zealous man may often lead him to the bigotry of fanaticism, for it shares the same root with jealousy. He sees the gloomy side, his imagination depicts the horrors of evil; and, alas for the people in his power, if to him evil means the non-acceptance of his theories of religious life. It is then that the blood of the martyr flows. While we can hardly imagine enthusiasm persecuting—it is too joyous. It will persist in seeing the hopeful side, and must needs evolve a theory that includes the salvation of everybody.

Among the many differences between the Hebrew and the Puritan, so often compared because of their likeness, we may specify this same difference. The Hebrew has ever been an optimist. His heart was full of hope and even persecution could never quite kill it. The dry study of the Talmud, even his diligent observation of ceremonials shows a religious enthusiasm in his playful interpretation. It was formalism tempered with humor. The Lord would always rebuild Zion, the throne of David would surely be exalted, the mountain of the Lord of Hosts would one day be established above the hills, and all the nations would flock to it. The historian calls the life of the Jew of the Middle Ages, a fifteen-hundred-year tragedy, but strange to say he himself was blissfully unaware of it. He even persuaded himself that he was the blest of mankind. The Jew never feared God, he trusted Him too implicity, he felt too near to Him, too certain of His protection. -

But to the Puritan life was an awful ordeal, and the
world a vale of tears. Joy was akin to sin, and virtue
was reached only through the torturing path of pain·
The ebullition of gladness must be discouraged, for evil
lurked at its root. Even art and beauty were frowned
upon. Religion meant suppression; evil preponderated
in man, and only by persistent denial of the innocent
joys of life could the kingdom of God be attained. The
Puritan is always a fine figure, but a gloomy one, and
his life looks better to us with the halo of distance over
it than it probably was to those who lived in its midst.
Woe to those who came under his righteous condemnation, it knew no pity. And the wife who forgot her
vows must publicly bear the letter of shame on her
breast in the scarlet color of guilt. We can understand
how the doctrines of Calvin came to be accepted as the
ways of God to man. Only a few could be elect-saved
in this world of sinfulness and folly. The jaws of hell
must be very wide and the flames of hell very fierce to
purge out the wickedness of depraved humanity.

Some are impatient with enthusiasm and distrust it.
They say it is another name for the ignorance of youth
that has not tasted the difficulties of life, that thinks all
things easy, because it has not found out their actual
conditions. There is a partial truth in this. When we
are very young, life seems an unbounded opportunity
and all our feverish dreams picture a bright, dazzling
future, in which everything is possible of accomplishment. As discretion comes with the years we learn how
narrow our sphere is after all, even in the infinities of
time and space. We find that environment shuts us
within a very limited circle of activity; and though it
seemed in the early days that we had an unconfined
choice of action and way of life, we look back upon it
and find that the path was all mapped out, that a destiny

was almost assigned to us, and that what seemed a free
choice was the inexorable consequence of circumstance.
And so, age, more sober, less trustful, hopes less, expects
less. ·It has come to understand the gap between expectation and realization. It does not look for surprises, is
does not anticipate revolutions for the morrow. It sees
the world run on in its sober course ; the great things
are not accomplished with great words, while the fiery
impetuosity of youth burns itself out. But let us not
confuse enthusiasm with the turbulence of madness or of
boyish ecstacy, even though we have compared it to fire.
Fire is constructive as well as destructive. It can warm
without burning. Its chief purpose is to sustain, only
its abuse is to consume. The fire lit by a soldier of Titus
burnt the Temple to ashes; but the holy lamp lit by the
victorious Maccabees illumed its precincts with soft and
mellow splendor, and became the symbol of hope and
faith and God's eternity for centuries after.

Let us not forget that the quiet glow that pervades the
soul as it daily does its work, while humbly recognizing its limitations after dreams of youth are past. that
feels the serene sway of divine protection ruling all
things for the wisest and best of ends, is enthusiasm also,
the more intense because it is suppressed to the dignified
gentleness of an outward calm. Enthusiasm need not
be impetuous or demonstrative, but if the gleam of faith
enlightens the face so that it shines as that of Moses
when he came down from the mount, and if the eyes,
those windows of the soul, tell us with their calm and
trustful look that all is well within, and the struggles
of life cannot move it from its confidence in the never-
ceasing providence of God—then have we enthusiasm in
its purest and most exalted form. It is the impulse
behind the faith that says "life is easy, because life is
good, whatever is—is right, the sad is only seeming."

There was another side to the Chanukah story that is perhaps not quite so well known. Before Antiochus, the tyrant, tried by force of arms to suppress a great religion, not knowing the power of ideas, a more subtle enemy was working insidious destruction within the fold. It was an age of religious indifference. In the words of Isaiah, "Those who should have led the people caused them to err," the priests had become worldly, and the office of high priest, a position of emolument, given to the highest bidder. You are told in the story how Antiochus defiled the Temple by offering swine's flesh on the altar, and erecting within it the statue of Jupiter Capitolinus. But these idolatrous symbols could not defile. Only when the fashionable brought their sacrifices correct in form according to the Levitical code, but with a perfunctory conventionality which showed that the spirit of worship was absent—*then* was the Temple defiled and God blasphemed. It was the repetition of an earlier condition denounced by the prophets as *ecclesiastically perfect and morally rotten.* Furthermore the unfortunate example of Greek immorality, like the example of Canaanite immorality in earlier days, came to be followed by the weak and the worldly. The sensual pleasures of Hellenic life, the barbarities of the amphitheatre, came for the first time to have a home in Jerusalem; the grand old faith was waning, the fires were very low and the light in the Temple was out spiritually before Antiochus extinguished it externally. These were the religious conditions ere a breath of persecution was perceptible. Then came the edict of the king: "Down with that alien faith. Let the gods of Greece be the gods of Judea." As a rod thrust into heated ashes stirs them into flame, so the antagonism of Antiochus awakened Israel from that lethargy that would have ended in religious death. The old fire leaped forth with new flashes, the Maccabean became the embodiment of religious revival. "Down with the heathen altar, down with the heathen immorlity ! Jehovah and righteousness forever !"

How beautifully the story is pictured in the symbol associated with it ! One light for the first night, two for the second, three for the third, until the eighth is reached. So the spark brightened to a glow and the glow lighted to a flame, and the flame spread to a conflagration as the electricity of religious enthusiasm ran through the ranks of Israel, and the light in their temple was but the external indication of the light in their hearts. They were once more a people irresistible, because they were a people glowing with the enthusiasm of religious fervor.

The fire of our faith is burning very low to-day ; a something of the apathy of the pre-Maccabean period is settling upon us. Religion does not mean a holy thing to us, but is rather like a relic which is preserved—the survival of a something whose force is spent and whose purpose is ended. A significant incident in the Maccabean struggle was that on one occasion, when the enemy came to attack our ancestors on the Sabbath day, they submitted to slaughter rather than desecrate its sanctity. And only after that did they deliberately decide that in future, when attacked on the Sabbath, they would consider themselves justified in resisting. Think of it, that men should deem it necessary to debate the question as to whether they dare desecrate their Sabbath, even in defending themselves against those who would slay them and their own ! Think of presenting such an alternative to the fin-de-siecle Jew as he is found in his spacious warerooms on Broadway, or loitering in the parlors of the Harmonie or the Progress ! Think of these material voluptuaries, who exhaust the good things of life and are indifferent to its ideals, coming to consider

whether they would be justified in defending their lives
if attacked on the Sabbath day !

➤ Everything is difficult to us. It is difficult to keep the
Sabbath; it is difficult to learn the language associated
with our faith; it is difficult to pray; it is difficult to
recognize the observances that mark the great events in
our great past; it is difficult to conform to the ceremonials that give symbolic realization to religious ideas.
All of these things are difficult, because there is no faith
in the religion that demands them. Enthusiasm fires
scepticism chills. Says the unbelieving and therefore
inactive squire to the believing and therefore fervent
Robert Elsmere : "I intend to put down enthusiasm."—
"What is the secret of your enthusiasm ?" said the
naturalist to Judah, the Welsh preacher. "I believe in
what I say." "So do I." "What did you lecture about
last ?" "Tadpoles." "I spoke about faith in the living
God." "What matters it,' said the Maccabeans, " if we
cannot worship God in our homes and in broad daylight, why, we can go down into the caves and worship
Him." And so they did. But that was the Maccabean
spirit. Religion was a real thing to them. There was
no doubt about it. Its demands were specific, certain:
its authority was undoubted.

Occasionally, when conscience-stricken at the unedi-
fying picture their religious anarchy must present to the
world at large, this latter-day generation points to the
minister, and holds him responsible for all its short-
comings, for all its demoralization, for the religious
confusion and the religious indifference that is their con
dition to-day, saying, perhaps, as Israel said to Moses :
"Wherever have you brought us to the wilderness to
slay us ?" We heard some such accusations last year in
this city, and again only recently from New Orleans.
Have the accusing laity ever thought of the humiliating

position of their ministers in feeling that they are teachers of a religion that is not believed, the shepherds of flocks that no longer care for their ministrations? Do they realize the bitterness of a profession that they treat as perfunctory and maintain with an indifferent nonchalance, as belonging to a something outside of their lives? Cicero did not know how two augurs could look in each other's faces without laughing; but with us *the people* laugh, or rather sneer, and bid their augurs, their ministers, be serious!

The lamp is burning very low indeed, and some are asking if the faith be dying. Will a Judas Maccabeas rise within our midst to rekindle the flame of enthusiasm, or must we wait for an Antiochus or a Pharaoh to come with the prod of persecution and sting us into life again?

You will not find much in the ancient codes against suicide. It is so opposed to our normal human nature, that the old legislators might well have felt it a question that would take care of itself. Penalties are imposed as preventions; and a man would hardly refrain from taking his own life, because, if unsuccessful, the State might take it for him. Nor would the awful condition of mind that would contemplate suicide be likely to dread a lesser punishment. But our codes of law have a further moral influence : we all shrink from doing that which the State calls a crime, independent of the punishment entailed. And when Religion and Law unite, as they do to-day, in condemning suicide, the thought of the disgrace one leaves behind may act as a wholesome deterrent.

We can find no distinct law against suicide in the Bible, although Genesis ix. 5, " The blood of your lives will I require," is sometimes so interpreted by the Rabbins. This text may be Shakespeare's authority for saying that the " Everlasting had set His canon 'gainst self-slaughter." Indeed, we only meet in the Scriptures with one actual case of suicide—that of Ahithophel the traitor, who hung himself when the bad cause he espoused seemed lost. For, when the dying Abimelech asks his attendants to slay him, so that he might not die by the hand of a woman, and when Saul on Gilboa, wounded to death, falls upon his sword, we can hardly consider either of these instances deliberate suicide.

At one period of Roman history—significantly the period of its decay—suicide was even encouraged and applauded. The bodies of criminals were exposed after death to public ignominy, and, their goods being confiscated, their children were reduced to poverty. But if they anticipated their death by suicide, the physical courage it was supposed to display was recompensed by the applause of the public, decent honors of burial and the right to will their property. To dispose of one's own life was conceded the natural rights of a citizen, and the stoics taught it as a part of their principles. And so the Roman, dissatisfied with his lot, or tired of life, worn out by his excesses, would open his veins in a warm bath, and that was the end of him.

The morals of religion have always connected murder and suicide very closely, and there is, of course, an obvious relation. Furthermore, whenever suicide is condoned, human life, as such, was deemed proportionately cheap. The Greeks, who permitted suicide, also encouraged parents to expose weak children, so that they would probably die. The East of to-day that bids the widow commit suttee, allows the father to drown superfluous daughters in infancy For it stands to reason, that if suicide be no crime, on the theory that the life is our own, then the taking of another life is wrong, chiefly because it is not our own, but murder, to be prevented, must be forbidden on graver grounds than that.

What is our attitude towards this question to-day? It has been recently brought to our notice by a letter from Mr. Ingersoll justifying suicide under certain conditions. We must at once waive from the discussion some of the instances brought forward by him as not really touching the question. When a person stands between two deaths—between, as he instances, fire and water--and chooses that which is the less painful, it is only playing with the question to call it suicide. There is no law that says if he happens to be standing in the flames

he shall abide there; with equal reason, we might call
the passive yielding to inevitable death—suicide. He is
equally evading the question when he classes martyrdom under this head. The martyr does not take his own
life; he stands by his convictions, though he knows
death will be imposed. He does not choose death; he
chooses to obey his conscience, no matter what may
happen. He fulfils his duty—that is, as far as he goes—
as to what consequences may follow that are beyond his
control, that is not his doing, nor need be his consideration, morally speaking; his persecutors may be mur-
derers, but he is no suicide. If a woman, according to
Jewish law, slay herself to save her honor, or the conscientious Hebrew dies rather than publicly worship an
idol, or rather than kill another, that is not suicide. He
is under compulsion; he is not permitted to follow his
or her duty unmolested; self-slaughter is forced upon
the individuals by the person who creates for them
this fearful alternative. It is his doing virtually, the act
of the victims only accidentally. As well call the soldier
a murderer, who, at call of duty, rushes upon certain
death—as well call the six hundred at Balaclava suicides, because the death of the majority was undoubted—
"It was theirs but to do—and die." No man who dies for
his country is a suicide; to call him such is to juggle
with language and to distort truth.

I would, therefore, exclude these instances that do not
legitimately enter the question—which is : Has an individual the right to take his own life, if he values it no
longer? Has he the right to deliberately avoid life,
purely on the ground of preference to be "rid of a
thousand natural shocks," to escape pain or trouble, or
the continuance of that which is disagreeable ?

I say we must not destroy our life, first, because it is not
ours absolutely to destroy. In our best moments, we feel

that we are, as it were, entrusted with our own souls, as a charge, to discipline and cultivate, to purify and enrich; that we belong to God, and because we are His creatures, therefore has He the authority to impose moral duties. We feel that certain things we may do and certain things we may not do, even though they do not affect our fellow-men. Not being the absolute possession of ourselves, but of Him we call our Maker, we are, therefore, account-able to Him for all we do. To destroy our life is to destroy a something which is not ours.

We must not destroy life, secondly, because little that we know of it, we know enough to be assured that it is sacred. It is not a chattel to be used as far as it may give pleasure, and then to be thrown away. There is nothing except God that is higher and holier than a human being. "I thank thee, Lord, that I am fearfully and wonderfully made." I must not play with this divine mechanism, whose secret is the secret of the whole universe. To lay hands upon my life, not knowing what it is, nor into the presence of what fate that act may usher me, is like a child touching a spring in the engine-room of a complicated machine, ignorant of the vast processes it may set in motion.

If I assume the right to destroy my life, I can surely do anything with it short of destroying it. I can throw it away in a lesser sense. I can abuse it, defile it, cor-rupt it. The right of suicide would eventually rule out all moral restraint. If I am justified in ending my life to save myself from pain, I can certainly drop my duties, cease my undertakings and my efforts—to save myself from pain—for these are all less than self-destruction, since that implies them all.

To end life to be free of trouble, is the absolute contra-diction of all religious teaching. The aim of life is not to be rid of trouble, nor even to secure happiness, though this may follow from righteous doing. Sometimes conscience tells us deliberately to impose suffering on ourselves. Not a day passes but what, in some instances, we turn from the easy and inviting to that which may be irksome and difficult, because our duty, our sense of right, our responsibilities, demand it. Accept a philosophy that we are justified in avoiding the disagreeable, and righteousness will be no more; man becomes a brute who

> Takes his lust in the fields of time,
> Unfettered by the sense of crime.

To attain great ideals men have readily renounced the world's joys and taken on the garb of woe; and thus plodding their hard way and heroically fighting many dangers, they have bravely held on till their release came, never laying down their hard lot while there was a breath in their body to speak a good word or strike a brave blow. They are the world's heroes, and from their lives we still draw helpfulness and inspiration to do our little duty, and bear our smaller woes uncomplainingly, cheerfully, manfully. It is hard to find a great man who has been a suicide, for that is the last example to teach us, we can make our lives sublime.

A man must not take his life because, further, he belongs to others. He belongs to his country. Each one of us is one of the units that is sustaining the vast and complicated machinery of production and distribution of law and order that comprise the activities of the country and are needed to keep alive and in proper mental and moral condition every soul within it. A man is worth a good deal more to his country than just that which would sustain himself, and therefore his death is a distinct loss. In our later productive years we are supposed to pay back what we owe from early years of youth, while we were being supported, but were doing nothing.

But we belong to our families in a much closer and in a
more real way than to the state or to society. The country
bears the loss, but the family feels it. For it is hard to
find an individual who has no ties, either ties to which he
is born or later ties that he makes by marriage. No man
liveth to himself. And he cannot suddenly vacate his
place without breaking many links, and leaving a sad void
in many hearts. For a man to acknowledge that he
stands utterly alone is in itself his own condemnation ;
it would imply what a completely selfish life his must be.
And for a woman to stand absolutely alone is unthink-
able; love is the very breath of her life.

Mr. Ingersoll cites the instance of a person suffering
from an incurable disease—a burden to himself, of
no use to others, where lengthening of life is but
lengthening of pain. I will begin by saying that because people have been willing patiently to continue
living and bearing their incurable diseases, has science
been encouraged and assisted in making some so-called
incurable diseases curable. The Homes for Incurables
show that life is worth living, even for the sick poor.
The victim on the sick-bed has his blissful hours, when
there is no pain, when love and tenderness are showered
upon him, when his surroundings are made cheerful and
his simple yearnings gratified. As to being a burden
instead of a use to others. I think we are apt to measure
all things by our material standards, and because the invalid is not making coats, because he is not earning his
board, therefore his life is not worth the care it costs to
those who love him. Are his children or his kin so
hardened that they will be glad to be rid of him —will his
death bring them no regret and no pain ? Whoever is
loved is of use, in the joy and comfort his presence gives
to those who love him. The lesson of patience and re-
signation that he teaches them may be more valuable

than $2 a day earned in traveling for watches or cigars.
The restraint his illness imposes on their pleasure and
the exercise of their spirits, the constant care and cost
that his ailment demands, which their sense of duty and
their feeling of affection and pity freely grant, tends to
enrich their characters and to purify them by thought
for others that is of distinct moral gain to the world. It
is just these obligations that prevent us degenerating into
brutes and beasts, that foster those tender and unselfish
traits in human nature that mark man's upward progress.

But see the danger of creating a sanction that justifies
one suffering from an incurable disease in "making his
quietus with a bare bodkin!" The next step will be to
commit suicide in an illness that might *perhaps* be incurable, and it soon becomes a question of degree, once the
thin end of the wedge is admitted, to seek relief in death
from all maladies that make life for the time being seem
not worth living. Create that sanction that justifies
self-murder in the case of extreme illness, and a stage
will be reached when the unscrupulous relatives, or even
misguided ones, may advise the step, may *assist* it themselves. Here is the subtle relation between suicide and
murder The next stage brings us back to the state of
the savage, who puts to death all his aged relatives when
too old and too weak to work and likely to become a
burden to themselves. When we recall, too, the work
that has been done on the sick-bed or in the invalid's
chair, between the hours of agony or even during them,
to allay the pain in occupation by the Heines, the
Scotts, the Stevensons and a thousand others. work
that has been precious inheritance richly treasured by
future generations.

The next instance of suicide's advocate is that of a
criminal detected in his crime, or a girl who has gone
the way of indirection, and both find disgrace and shame

staring them in the face. It is rather difficult to decide in how far the justification of suicide would weigh with those who are themselves transgressors. But presuming that they are not so lost to the qualms of conscience, but that they would hesitate to slay themselves if self-slaughter were called a crime, then I think that that very sense of compunction within them would show that there are possibilities of retrieval, that in their cases, at least, it is not too late to mend. And they have before them, too, the encouraging example of men who had stooped to crime, of women who had forgotten the holiness of their womanhood, who, repenting the rash step, had yet lived to be useful and respected members of society.

Another instance is the man who has failed in business, or, what is worse still, in life. He is brought to the verge of despair, his hopes are blasted, his mercantile reputation gone. In the conflict for existence he is worsted; the odds are against him. Is it right that a man should incur the responsibilities of a wife and children, and then, when trouble comes, to leave them in the lurch? We have not words hard enough for a man who runs away and deserts his wife and children? But what is this? Why ask them to bear the burden alone, added to the disgrace of his suicide, so that his name can only be mentioned in the family under the breath? And should he not consider what it means to lose a husband or a father at one sudden blow, without a word of preparation? What right has he to impose that misery on them, and, to escape his own troubles, to make at one blow his wife a widow and his children fatherless? Is there any form of cowardice more outrageous? Thousands of others have bravely borne the loss of wealth, the ruin of business, have faced poverty for the first time late in life, and have even lived to emerge from it once more; and if not that, to adapt themselves heroically to the new conditions and make the best of them. A woman is always ready to adapt herself to the new and humbler life—that is her history. I can imagine a bereft wife crying in her agony when the awful news comes: "O, would that you had stayed with us to cheer us, so that we might have borne the burden together! Widowhood and orphanage are harder than poverty; rather a crust with you than luxury with out you!"

And as to him who thinks himself a failure, of no use in the world, a spoiled cipher that may be well cast out, we can surely always do something better with our lives than destroy them. Do you stand there and say there is not a bit of use you can make of your life, that it is worthless, like the garbage we dump into the sea? You have organs, senses, capacities—as a piece of machinery merely, you are valuable; and if there be but a spark of good left in you to direct those energies, dare you to say you are of no use whatever? To say that is the most awful reproach you can hurl against God—as though one would say to the Almighty, "Behold one of your failures, Sir!"

That we cannot justify suicide either by religion or by law does not say that we do not pity the suicide. It is awful to think of one brought to that degree of desperation where life is unsupportable, recognizing that self-preservation is the first law of nature. We all know how unhappy even small things can make us at times, "that a prick of a pin will make an empire insipid." We know that every life, in some measure, has its bitterness, its hardships, its miseries, its sufferings. There are moments of agony when the oppressed soul cries out, "My anguish is too great to be borne!" But just because we know there are counterbalancing joys, that the moments of extreme woe do not last, that we even look back upon them surprised and sometimes ashamed that we should have succumbed so easily—for that very reason. we do not wish to encourage, by the endorsement of religion and law, a rash step from which there is no retreat, taken in an irresponsible moment of despair. For no man of those who have held the pistol to their heads and have refrained in time but has blessed his self-restraint in after-years, when joy came back again, and he finds himself a useful member of society, in the midst of a loving family circle, who never know of that one dark moment that might have left its blighting shadow upon them for years to come.

And I really believe that a larger number of suicides are the worn-out roués who have no cares, no duties, no responsibilities, disgusted with life because they have done no good with it, and have thrown it away virtually before they do so actually.

I cannot begin to tell you the awful danger to society of justifying suicide, nor where the tendency would lead. To justify a step is to legitimatize it ; and when a man may calmly consider, "Shall I commit suicide?" as though he consider, "Shall I enter a profession? shall I marry?" the sense of moral obligation that holds society together would snap, and Rome's fate would be ours.

If we evaded our difficulties by self-destruction, man would accomplish nothing. He has risen step by step to higher planes of achievement only by not permitting himself to be mastered by obstacles, to be deterred by dangers, to be disheartened by defeats. By not giving up the struggle when the miseries came has he wrung physical and spiritual triumphs from those miseries.

We believe in life, in its inherent good, and in its grand, limitless possibilities, and therefore we wish to put around it all the safeguards possible. We wish to teach our young that life means duty ; it is a sacred treasure entrusted to our care, and that we must make the worthiest use of it ; that it is not a plaything or a toy to be preserved only so long as it may give us pleasure, but, as a great philosopher has said, it is a fort with which we are instructed, and, like good, brave, dutiful soldiers, we must not capitulate, whatever happens. until the summons comes from the Great Commander.

"And God said unto Abraham, Take now thy son, thine only son, whom thou lovest—Isaac, and offer him up for a burnt offering. And Abraham rose early and saddled his ass, and took two of his young men with him and Isaac his son, and he clave the wood for the burnt offering. . . . And Isaac said unto his father, Behold the fire and the wood, but where is the lamb for the burnt offering? And Abraham replied, God will provide himself a lamb for the burnt offering. And Abraham built an altar and bound Isaac his son and laid him on the altar, and stretched forth his hand and took the knife to slay his son. And an angel of the Lord called to him out of heaven and said, Lay not thy hand upon the lad, nor do anything to him, for now I know that thou fearest God, seeing that thou hast not withheld thy son, thine only son from me." (Gen. xxii.)

Before entering upon our theme proper, let us begin by replying to those who see in this chapter, from its historical side, nothing but the narrative of impossible marvels, which our reason tells us must be fabulous, and, from its religious side, nothing but the illustration of idolatrous form of worship—human sacrifice, which civilized humanity has long since outgrown. In meeting the first conclusion, it is unnecessary for me to say to those familiar with my attitude of belief, that I do not ask you to believe that the Almighty or his angelic messenger appeared in the heavens and spoke to Abraham from the clouds. Without entering into details, you know that it conflicts absolutely with our conception of God's omnipresence and spirituality, and with our knowledge of Nature's laws. But you should also know that there is a wide gulf between believing in the Bible records as exact scientific and historic statements on the one hand, and, on the other, rejecting the book altogether as untrustworthy, not deserving our veneration and respect.

We have learned to read the Bible in a new way. We

are beginning to enter into the spirit of the ancient writers. We find they did not write history first, then drawing morals from it; they wrote morals first, and myth as well as fact was then brought into service to illustrate and vivify the moral. In these illustrations, we can here and there pick up valuable bits of history, but the so-called historical books are not histories as we use that word to-day. It is one sphere for the archæological critic to examine this chapter of Abraham's trial of faith, and, by comparing it with contemporary documents—if there be any—and studying the usages and morals of the age, so completely to sift the story as to be able to give us, with a fair amount of certainty, the actual occurrence. It is entirely another sphere for the religious teacher to find out the purpose for which the chapter was written, and to guage not only the moral intent of the writer, but also its moral tone from our own standard. Much of the misunderstanding and abuse of the Bible has arisen from a confusion of two spheres of Scripture s udy as distinct as that of the surveyor who measures a piece of land into acres, locating its rock and its marsh, and the poet who, stirred by the beauty of the stretch of landscape before him, sees in its dateless hills and crumbling rocks the footprints of God.

With this new spirit there has come to us a new reverence for the Bible, and a new appreciation of its preciousness, and we lovingly read over the old stories, and see how much more they mean than the actual fact related, even if absolutely authentic; and that, entirely independent of the added credibility that the unearthing of cuneiform monuments may give to some Bible stories in Genesis and Kings; they convey life lessons that seem to persist through all man's changing views; and amidst the upheaval of old systems and beliefs and social evolution, they abide as the eternal truths.

"Still, why go back to the Bible?" some progressive schools are persistently asking? " We are wiser to-day than the men who wrote it. Their views of life and of all things were limited, and we ourselves can see their limitations. See how far the world has advanced in all directions from the standards of Solomon and Jehu. Why go back to them?"

Among the many things that we are learning from the light that is coming in from all directions, one great truth is, that the intellectual gulf between antiquity and our own times is largely a mirage. Humanity is one ; duty is one. The conditions of life are the same, and each age wrestles with the same religious problems, even while they worshiped strange gods. Make the setting old Chaldea if you like, or make it bran new Chicago, the trial and the temptations that came to Abraham on Mount Moriah come to us. He wore a turban and rode an ass; we wear a Paris hat and travel on the "flier," but beneath these externals the man is the same. Material civilization has not taught man to subdue his passions, and varied versions of David's sin with Bath-Sheba are given us in every morning's newspaper, not as occurring among the criminal and ignorant exclusively either, but among the social leaders of the world. We have improved our methods of executing criminals, it is true; but Cain and Absalom still kill their brothers for jealousy or revenge.

Aristotle stated some fundamental philosophical truths 350 years before the common era, and no modern philosopher, not even Kant, has transcended him or advanced beyond some of his deductions. A recent writer dares to claim that we are not the intellectual superiors of the Greeks to-day; and a great French novelist has just said that the best things have already been written; that modern originality is but a literary writhing. Yes, the Bible is an old book, containing some conclusions which we have outgrown. But the Bible also contains certain grand ethical principles that are told in its pages once and for all time, and they make that book—amidst the million volumes daily printed—the one book of humanity for all ages.

I. Some of those eternal principles, as contained in this chapter. What are they? First, God does not accept human sacrifice as a form of worship, but he *does* ask the readiness and the willingness to make any sacrifice that our conscience tells us He demands. It is not the story of the sacrifice of Isaac, as it is sometimes loosely styled, for Isaac was not sacrificed; it is the trial of Abraham's faith. Do not be in too much of a hurry to condemn all ancient sacrifice as ignorant and cruel and wrong. These epithets may apply to the methods, but not to the idea of sacrifice as such. I say that God does ask sacrifice of us; that is one of the great demands of religion. The rationalists are in a dreadful hurry to stigmatise whatever does not touch their sentiments or come up to their point of view, as superstitious. Be the act what it may, if the spirit was reverent, it was raised above mere superstition. While, on the other hand, even our rational theories and catch-words can become superstitions and fetiches when we expect to do too much with them. It is not quite fair to primitive man to say that only a selfish desire for protection or a cowardly fear of harm prompted the first sacrifice. I do not believe it. I rather see a faint glimmer of the sense of obligation to some Higher Unknown, a conscientious scruple against gratifying every desire, a feeling, however perverted in its blundering application, that self-denial is a needed discipline, that we should give up our very nearest and dearest, just because they are our dearest.

II. To Abraham came in this same chapter a second revelation—a great revelation indeed—viz., that this spirit of denial could be carried to the extreme of sin, as all virtues carried to extreme are sins, that the sacrifice of a human life cannot be acceptable to God, since, in the first place, it involved a crime—murder ; and since, secondly, no one individual is the absolute property of another to do with as he will; that even our children are not possessions for our absolute keeping, but only charges entrusted to our care.

You will remember Abraham sacrifices a ram in place of the boy, implying that this was a form of worship more acceptable to God.   He had not reached the point of seeing the grossness even of animal sacrifice—that revelation came to later teachers—the prophets.   One man cannot grasp all truth at once.   But even here you will notice what a slighting attention is given to this offering of the ram as of some ceremonial detail aside from the great question at issue—which was the readiness of Abraham to yield up what was to him most precious in life at what he thought was the call of duty.

III. Sacrifice is a necessary feature of life.   Self-denial is the child's first lesson.   Not that we should sacrifice merely for the sake of sacrifice—that is wanton, whether it be the human or animal sacrifices of antiquity, or the asceticism and monasticism of mediævalism, or the harsh restrictions of Puritanism nearer our own times.   Life's legitimate sacrifices will always be found involved in its duties.   We must first decide what our duty is, and then fulfil it, involve what sacrifices it may, but we must not first begin with the sacrifice, just for the sake of making it, and call that duty.   Such is artificial, and leads to endless useless restrictions hampering the free play of our spirits, restricting our lawful pleasures, checking our activities, and needlessly saddening our lives. Such, too, is the fundamental error of Christianity in teaching on the ancient theory that an arbitrary sacrifice of an individual is necessary to save the world from sin; hence the doctrine of their crucified Messiah, instead of teaching that for each separate individual, salvation from sin can only be won by sacrificing the gratifications that cause sin. The world is not saved by the sacrifice of one good man, but by the sacrifice of the bad in all men.

IV. Sacrifice is involved in religion; we cannot be religious unless we have the sacrificing spirit. "Thou asketh not animal sacrifice, else would I give it; but the sacrifice of a contrite heart thou wilt not despise." Religion should never impose arbitrary sacrifice, be it the giving of sheep, money, candles, or the self-imposition of flagellation, penances, pilgrimages or poverty. Religion must concern itself entirely with the work of bringing man to God and making him godlike, but in its practical application in human life this will imply great sacrifice. We must coerce the will in righteous directions, we must subdue the passions, tearing out our carnal appetites with torturing wrench until the heart sweats tears of blood. Is not that sacrifice—do you know a greater? Does only Jacob wrestle at night with the mysterious messenger, who being conquered becomes an angel and bestows a blessing on his foe? Is not this a law of our being vividly put in this mythic form? Does the temptress of lust come only to Joseph, bidding him betray his master, dishonor himself and defy his God? "No longer human sacrifice to-day—surely?" Not arbitrary human sacrifice, but when duty involves the laying down of life, not for the sake of the life but for the sake of the duty, what then? Our rabbinical code answers the question in no uncertain language. On three alternatives must we yield our life—first, when the alternative is idolatry, and every martyr in our roll of merit has obeyed this law, and those in Spain who evaded it are called Marranos, accursed; second, on the alternative of dishonor—and a striking example is the wife of Rabbi Moses ben Hanoch, who threw herself in the sea to escape defilement thereby; on the alternative of murder—when one is asked to slay another under the threat of being slain himself. And so I say to you: *Do* sacrifice your children; your "only son," your beloved daughter, when it is a choice between their worldly success and your moral integrity, and give them a crust and honor rather than a cushioned seat, that has cost too much because it has cost the sacrifice of right. Do not make their welfare excuse for your degeneration. But if they be old enough, gather them about you and tell them you can win that which will bring much emolument, but it will involve dishonor, not perhaps to the knowledge of men, but in the knowledge of conscience and of God. Don't fear for the children; you will find them as ready as Abraham found Isaac to yield his life to what he thought was the call of God and Duty. Their welfare indeed—"a good name is an inheritance to one's children's children."

V. Now I am brought to ask a direct question : Are we religious people, deriving religion from *religare* self-restraint? Do we make the sacrifices that religion involves, or do we stop short the moment it asks a sacrifice? The religious test only begins, then, as Abraham's did. To be a consistent Jew of any school implies many an act of abnegation and self-denial. When principle conflicts with interest, with expediency, with pride, what do you do? Do you sacrifice your material advantage, or do you sacrifice your principles?

There were daily sacrifices in the ancient Temple, as there are daily sacrifices in modern life. You know what they are. They come up in the home, in relations with wife, children, domestics, tradesmen ; they come in your office, be it a professional or a commercial one, or but a humble shop: they come up in society, be it the society of the Knickerbockers or of the Ghetto ; they enter into the consideration of the clothing you should wear, the food you eat, the books or papers you choose to read, and very largely, of course, in your amusements and recreations. Some lives are all indulgence. See the bloated, dissipated creature, with his abused life written in his face, like the brand of Cain, so that every one who sees him knows him ! Some lives, again, are all sacrifice. See the gentle, spiritual nature, with all human craving subjected, the face transfigured with a holy rapture ! But within these two extremes, between which most of us fall, we meet every degree of sacrificing character, and we can usually read the story of people's lives when we look at them.

God's law of sacrifice is, then, that we should yield up the lower for the sake of the higher, so that sacrifice is not a loss, but a gain. Our lives need enriching by denial. Emancipation, prosperity, may have materialized us. "Jeshurun waxed fat and kicked." Are not we modern Jews learning to philosophize away our religious obligations? I fear the taint of epicureanism has touched us. Religion is subordinated to the most trivial convenience of life, and, therefore, ceases to be religion. We *have* too much ; we *are* too little. Greatness lies not in what you possess, but in what you can renounce. Diogenes found that a tub was the only article of furniture necessary for his life, that, having two hands, even a drinking-cup was unneeded.

VI. One more religious principle does this great chapter teach us. "God will provide the sacrifice," says Abraham to Isaac; and God did provide, the story goes on to tell us, and this fact gives a name to the place יהוה יראה "The Lord will provide." When we say that all that we have we receive from God, we usually have in mind our material blessings. We lose sight of the fact that our spiritual resources are His gift also. With the bestowal of blessings there is granted also, in varying degrees, the power of renunciation—more precious to our higher life than the blessing itself, if we only knew. It is awful to give up what we love. It would seem as though our mortal being could not bear the wrench, and yet the power comes—the back broadens to the burden, the soul steadily rises to the height of its responsibilities, the spirit deepens and strengthens to its sufferings God has concealed His healing for our woes in the woes themselves. Thus in the very giving we gain moral power and character. God returns our offerings a hundredfold. Sacrifice enricheth, while indulgence impoverisheth. The bread cast on the waters returns after many days. We sow the seed in tears, we reap the sheaves in joy. This is religion's law.

God asks the sacrifice, provideth it Himself. And after it is given, we find the dross has gone; the best and dearest abounds—now doubly dear because of our spirit of abnegation.

Will God's saving-power be manifested at humanity's supreme hour of need? Verily, even at the moment when hope is darkest, as surely as the stars will move in their courses, "will God provide." The heavens open, so to speak, at the fatal moment, the Divine reassurance comes, the shadow is lifted, and all is well. All may not happen as we would wish it, nor does the deliverance come always as clearly as the old story tells us it came to Abraham. But in His own wise way; which we must learn to understand is ever the best way, in His own good time, which is always the best time, will all our doubts and fears and pangs melt in the rising light of God's love for His creatures, which endureth forever and forever.

SELF-IMPOSED WOES OF LIFE.

No religion or philosophy has ever been able to explain away the woes of life; and Zeno, the founder of the school of stoicism, who denied the reality of pain, committed suicide when his own revolting experience contradicted his own theory. However much a Berkeley may deny the world of matter and declare that all is mind, even he does not attempt to doubt the actuality of suffering. Whatever be our different standpoints, we all recognize life's tragedies, we all recognize the genuineness of the sorrow that bereavement must bring, that failure must bring, that physical suffering must bring. As to what purpose these real woes may serve in life, as to the blessing that may be behind the tears, I will not now consider. My theme to-night is the self-imposed woes of life,—our fancied ills.

What is the distinctive characteristic of our era ? More than it is the age of invention, of electricity, or of iron, I think, it is the age of reflection. We look at the world and we ask: What is it? We look at ourselves and we ask: Whence have we come, why are we here, whither are we tending? The ancients did not ask these questions, or at least they left them to a few philosophers. They felt that they had been placed here for reasons best known to God and it was theirs but to fulfil here the duties that authority demands and that conscience endorses. Indeed, the majority of the people of the past did not even go as far as that statement. These questions did not suggest themselves at all, did not even come up to be suppressed. Men and women did not think of these things. They thought less and they lived more. They accepted their burdens as matter of course.

They saw and understood what they could, and they trusted God for the rest. "The hidden things belong to God, the revealed things belong to us and our children."

But our contemporaries have grown morbid. They are holding reflectors before them to watch the workings of their own souls. They torture themselves into doubt and conjure up gloomy possibilities. They love to question the fundamentals. Like Descartes, they put away all knowledge from them and try to reach it afresh through their own researches.

Very few have the sweeping grasp of an Aristotle or a Herbert Spencer to comprehend a cosmos, to imagine a world-system; so while they have successfully destroyed their faith and strengthened their doubts, they have left themselves nothing but a world of chaos with a blank behind and darkness beyond. All the people who are asking themselves the question: "Is life worth living?" with the invariably negative reply, have all reached that unhappy attitude by this morbid introspection, by this indulgence in the luxury of doubt, by giving rein to a despondent imagination.

Life is sad to very many, not because of its conditions, not because of their circumstances, not because of any physical suffering or worldly disappointment; but because they have individually formed a gloomy view of life's purposes, because they have questioned its inherent good, and doubted its righteous aim. Mental suffering is usually more acute than bodily suffering, and Job feels more pain when he doubts God's justice than he feels from all the stings of physical affliction. What consolation is there in a fine stud and $30,000 a year if the world came into existence by blind chance and by blind chance will one day drift into the sun to be consumed in its fires ?

We are subjective creatures, that is to say, we make

our own world, we decide our own happiness, our own misery. Anything can give us pleasure or give us pain, if our nature and our disposition so decide; temperament largely helps to give reality to happiness or misery. The awful horrors of Hell that damped the world's spirits for centuries were purely creations of imagination. You may recall the dialogue between the morbid, despondent Hamlet and the light-hearted Rosencrantz. "Denmark is a prison," declares Hamlet. Rosencrantz: "We think not so, my Lord." Hamlet: "Why, then, this none to you; for there is nothing either good or bad but thinking makes it so. To me it is a prison."

Look back into your lives and notice by what arbitrary rulings of our spirit cheer and despondency alternately obtain control. You are sitting quite still, when suddenly a thrill of joy surges through you at the mere delight of living. Or, again, you wake up one morning and you feel a depression that you cannot explain. You say you have the "blues." You recall the work before you; and the daily duties that you may have anticipated on another occasion with complacency, on this day you look forward to it with a something of dread. You feel a strange nervousness pervading your whole system that makes you exaggerate the slightest set-back; so overwrought have your feelings become, simply because of your condition, and not at all because of your circumstances, that the slightest jar will cause your feelings to overflow, will make you swear, if you are a man, or cry, if you are a woman. You recall an innocent something that one whom your fancy has made into an enemy had uttered, and the guileless utterance, coming back to your memory, takes new and distorted shape, until your morbid condition has magnified it into a colossal wrong. So your diseased fancy plays pranks with your feelings, and you succeed in reducing yourself

to a condition of abject misery simply out of the airy
nothings of your own imagnation. You look back later
with surprise and shame upon your own absurdity. While
I never wish to give into the theory that the physical
controls the moral, undoubtedly it largely influences it.
A chronic indiges ion may help us to doubt the immortality of the soul, while a low vitality may make one a
disciple of Schopenhauer. Meet such ailments on their
own grounds. Physical culture will certainly dispel
morbidness. Shun confinement and solitude, and when
the evil spirit is upon you go out into God's sunshine—
go among your friends. The contact with humanity is
the best elixir for many woes, imaginary and real.

I read recently that one of the differences between man
and the brute creation is that man is the only creature
that adorns himself with external ornament. Man, too,
has been called the "laughing animal" by way of distinction; but I think a fundamental difference also lies in the
fact that man is the only creature who anticipates, who
works for a future, rather than a present, who lays plans
for the morrow. This is undoubtedly a prime cause of
his great superiority and of his advances in what is called
civilization. But there is a sad extreme to this power of
anticipation. It is well that he should be able to look
into the future and provide for the wants of a distant
day, but when that precaution deepens into anxiety that
takes away the pleasure of the present joy, because of
the possibility of a future woe, then what had been a
faculty of growth becomes a useless cause of torment.
You are all familiar with the words, "to borrow trouble,"
and perhaps all of you at one time or another have been
guilty of that unprofitable, unbusiness-like negotiation.
Though you may never have to return the principal, or
even to to make use of it, the interest that you pay in
anxiety and in distress far outweighs the loan itself.

Some mothers, who have their unhappy faculty, make their children a source of pain to themselves instead of source of joy.

I think I may be safe in saying that our greatest troubles *never happen*, and that our greatest suffering comes from the troubles that might have been, that we thought possibly would happen, but which, as a matter of fact never did. We cross our rivers before we reach them, like Israel at the Red Sea, whose distressed imagination already saw their graves in the wilderness; while if we would but "journey forward," our knowledge and activity would show how fancied are the dangers. While we should not show a wanton disregard of impending danger, still, having provided for the "rainy day," as far as we can, then I say "we should drink and be merry, for to-morrow we *wont* die."

But I think that most of the worries of life come from the meannesses and the unworthiness of our own nature. Jealousy has probably caused more pain than poverty or physical suffering. Some one has said that it exacts the hardest service and pays the bitterest wages. "All my honors avail me nothing," says Haman, "while I see Mordecai sitting at the king's gate." And so, you may be comfortable, you may have all that the needs of life demand and much to supply its comforts; all is well at the office, your securities are safe, your returns are all that you would wish; the physician's carriage is not waiting at your door when you come home, the children and all dear to you are well; you have no real anxiety. But your acquaintance across the street has attained a commercial opportunity that had not come to you. The green-eyed monster pours gall into your cup of life and takes away its cheer. Ah, if we all could but obey the tenth commandment, and not "envy our neighbor's house," how much happier we would be! We deliberately make ourselves sad, not because of the lack of the things that we need, but because of the lack of the things that some one else has, the need of which we had never felt until he had come into possession. ."The soul of Jonathan was knit to the soul of David;" why,—for a reason that would have made a mean jealous nature hate David —for in the glare of David's success, Jonathan's lesser achievement was dimmed and forgotten. But Jonathan knew not the meaning of jealousy; he loved valor and loved it not the less when it eclipsed his own.

I remember reading in the press some time ago of quite a little tempest in a tea-pot that had occured between two Mrs. Astors at Newport, each claiming the privilege of being *the* Mrs. Astor, par excellence, to whom that title without any initial would be all-sufficient for the Post-Office; and it seemed strange and even wicked to think that people who had so much of this world's goods; who had but to press a button and Aladdin's thousand slaves appeared to do their bidding, should have indulged in this discontent and unsisterly feeling about such a triviality.

What a shallow, cramped, small world theirs must have been, after all.

What some people need is a real trouble to dispel their fancied ones.

A fine nature is never jealous. It realizes that every life has its short-comings and every life its compensation; and to be unhappy at not possessing that which may be possessed by another reveals a mean spirit, it is the under-valuing of one's own individuality, the absence of true self-respect. And, after all—if we only knew—our imagination accompanies the possession of certain advantages with an added happiness that never comes. We adjust ourselves to what we may possess, however much or little it may be, so that beneath all differences of rank and means, happiness preserves a pretty steady level all through.

There are many women who fain would win distinction in literature who are simply humble mothers of homes. I know a lady who has earned that coveted distinction, who has written many books, whose articles are accepted by the best magazines, who has won a reputation as a lecturer and who has a still more brilliant literary future before her; and yet I know there is a thorough disgust and discontent in her heart at the sadness of her lot, and that she would gladly and joyfully exchange her wordly fame to be the mother of one of the same humble homes where she in turn is the object of envy. 'Tis but the old story of the people who came to Jupiter to change their lot. "Choose what you will," he said. How soon they came back, pleading for their old burdens. We only see others' lives from the outside. You watch a woman who has become a leader of society, whose five-o'clock teas appear in the society items, whose gowns are quoted as authorities, who, of the world of fashion has become queen and whose drawing-room is the centre for celebrities. A thousand women who peer enviously into her card-receiver, yearn with a sickening longing for her exalted place. Do you know what that place has cost her and is costing her? A great deal more than it is worth.

How largely the woes of most of the great men in letters have been due to their own meanness, to their own bad nature, to their own cramped souls! Jonathan Swift, one of the unhappiest of litterateurs, whose life closed in the darkness of madness, turned his own heart to gall through hatred of his fellow-men. The vanity that begat dishonesty in Chatterton brought about his own suicide. Byron was disgusted with life, because he made life disgusting. Herder's jealousy of Goethe robbed him of his peace of mind. The meanness of Pope gave him many sad hours, and the intolerant jealousy of Voltaire that could brook no others' success made him a misanthrope and embittered his days. Because an inferior writer was preferred to him for a passing moment he almost went into the frenzy of despair. A great historian has said "he lacked the magnanimous patience of Milton that could leave his claims to the unerring judgment of time." Bacon, wisest and meanest of mankind, brought down his grey hairs in sorrow to the grave.

The desire to hold the very first place, the very highest seat, the desire that our name should always head the list, this is but an ignoble, even a vulgar, ambition. "I would sooner," said Cæsar, "be the first man in that little village, than the second man in all Rome." Alas for that unhappy and unworthy sentiment—it brought disaster to his country, and eventually caused his own downfall. There is a legitimate and an illegitimate ambition, and it was by the latter that the angels fell.

At times, it is true, we are distressed on righteous grounds. It pains us to see dishonesty enthroned in high places, to see the success of unscrupulousness, to find that a sham passes for the reality, and the very worldly qualities that our best nature must condemn becoming the means of earning popular admiration. And yet, this righteous indignation is after all not always righteous. For, if we would be true to our own standard of intrinsic worth, then we must measure even worldly success by the same standard and despise it together with the comtemptible methods that win it. If we value the good, then we must value it for itself and independent of any human or substantial rewards: and if, in our heart of hearts, we truly think moral excellence the highest excellence and the only excellence, then surely we should

be able to look with equanimity upon the association of
moral depravity and material prosperity. Yonder is a
lecturer, made famous by sensational methods, by adver-
tising himself as though he were a soap or a liver-pill.
Do you want that fame at that price? There is a multi-
millionare who wrecked a railroad and impoverished a
hundred widows; but he succeeded and the crowd gives
him adulation. Do you want that adulation—would it
not be to you as unwelcome as the contumely of the
worthy? Goodness is not a means but an end. "Fret
not thyself, because of evil-doers," says the Psalmist,
"neither be thou envious against workers of iniquity;
trust in the Lord, and verily thou shalt be sustained. Fret
not because of him who prospereth in his way, because
of the man who bringeth wicked devices to pass; cease
from anger, forsake wrath; fret not thyself in anywise to
do evil. The little that the righteous man hath is better
than the riches of any wicked." Is not this a philosophy of life? Enlarge your souls, rise above the petty
worries and petty ambitions of weak natures. "Hitch
your wagon to a star." Remember that some of the
world's greatest failures are life's best successes; and if we
really succeed in the higher aims of life, we can look with
equanimity upon our failure in the lower aims. It is so
easy to realize this truth in the distant perspective of
history—so hard to grasp it at the hour! Jeremiah
stays with the defeated, woe-begone brethren who had
misunderstood and persecuted him, and refuses the offer
of the King of Babylon of a post of ease and luxury.
Josephus deserts his brethren in the hour of their downfall, and accepts the honors of his country's enemy.
And till the end of time, posterity will love the one and
scorn the other.

After the great fire of Chicago, there were some houses
that put out the sign, "All lost but honor;" but if that

were saved and if it were valued, did not life still offer many bright promises? But lacking honor and then losing all material possessions, is he not "poor indeed?" And the loss brings no compensation to lessen the bitterness of its woe. Enlarge your souls, I say, and learn to look with a serene nature upon the set-backs and the crosses and the worriments that are woven into the woof of our life. Learn to live in the loftier realms of that larger generosity that feels friendliness to all mankind, that cannot stoop to gnawing jealousy or debasing hatred, but looks with pity, but without anger, upon the silly machinations of man for trifling superiorities and gains.

I remember once, when a minister was ordained to succeed a very eminent divine, that the clergyman who presided encouragingly said to the young man: "You need not be troubled at the thought as to whether you may ever be able to fill the place of your predecessor. You have not to fill his place: you have to fill your own." Let us not fret ourselves that we do not attain to the eminence or the opulence of this one or that, but measure ourselves only by the eternal standards, and try, with the help of God and the good-will of man, to do our duty here, to fulfil the mission that we feel is ours, to live up to the destiny that we find marked out for us, and to develop to the fullest all our powers.

CONSCIENCE AND EDUCATION.

What is conscience? Sometimes it is defined as the voice of God within us. This, however, is not a definition but only a figure of speech, and no figures are more unreliable than figures—of speech. Is not reason also called "the voice of God" in a popular maxim?

Conscience is a power of our being that discovers moral law; and since moral knowledge is the highest known to our experience, conscience that discovers it is the highest and noblest of our powers. Conscience is the superintendent of our actions, and passes a decision favorable or unfavorable on all we do.

This power is inherent in our nature. It is not an after-development, nor the result of education, though education can direct it and bring it to fruition. Education can train the eye; but sight is born with the human being. The infant is not taught to see—it sees; and if it be blind no teaching can give it sight. What is education? What but (*educo*) bringing forth—a something already there. So this conscience that finds out duty and realizes obligation is a power that in a higher or lower degree, is part of our human inheritance.

I said conscience discovers moral law, that is, it discriminates between our actions, our motives and our feelings, by calling some good and some bad. What conscience dictates is called—duty. It will approve of truth, justice, kindness; it will condemn falsehood, deceit, cruelty. Still the human being may form a mistaken conception of truth, of kindness, even of right. For conscience knows nothing of details, it only reveals general principles. It knows that we must seek the right and abstain from wrong. What is right, and what is wrong? In each instance, these are questions left to the education through experience. Perverted teachings can then so distort the conscience as to lead it to regard certain wicked things as honorable and some worthiness as shameful. In these instances conscience does not make the mistake, but the wrong education that misdirected it.

Conscience is always true to whatever standard of right our united experience creates. It always tells us to do what is believed to be right at the time. But since our ideas of right and wrong have undergone great change, so the dictates of conscience to-day may suggest to us duties the very reverse of those of another age. The crimes of one epoch may be the virtues of an earlier one.

For instance, among savages duty is confined usually to the members of the tribe. No duties are supposed to apply to people outside of it. On the contrary, it is considered even meritorious to do them an injury. Mistaken idea of duty impels the Indian widow to sit on the funeral pyre of her husband and be burnt to death with his body. The Festival of Venus represented to woman as a religious duty, what we would call by no other name than pollution. We find even Socrates, the supreme moral philosopher of Greece, teaching that it is our duty to do the greatest good we can to our friends and the greatest harm to our enemies. Sometimes fanaticism and ignorance will so befog the reason as to represent even cruelty as duty. Instances of this we find in the outrages of the Spanish Inquisition, the Auto de Fe, human sacrifices, "holy" massacres and "holy" wars.

Duty, furthermore, is relative. In the days when prisoners of war were put to death, the suggestion that they be made slaves instead was not cruel, but humane indeed. It was distinctly a step higher in moral conception. Slavery for that age meant progress: but slavery for this age has been rightly termed, "the sum of all villanies."

We find in the Bible the institution of Cities of Refuge. What purpose did they serve? It had been considered the duty of the nearest relative to avenge the blood of his kin by killing the slayer of his relative, even though the deed were accidental. The Mosaic code here endeavors to suppress the cruel custom that time had sanctioned, by the appointment of Refuge Cities, whither the slayer by accident might flee. Vendetta is still almost a religious duty among Corsicans, and the Mafia attempted to transplant it here.

The need of preserving the tribe against the encroachment of enemies raised the slaying of enemies into the most praiseworthy of deeds. Conscience dictated that it was the duty of each to destroy as many as possible; and bravery was not only exalted to the highest place among the virtues,—it was actually made *the* virtue, for that word goes back to a Latin root meaning bravery. Thus the heroes of the past were Achilles, Samson, Ulysses and Alexander. Their deeds hardly awaken to-day the admiration felt for them in olden times. And those too whom an earlier age sanctified as saints, we might condemn as barbarians.

Holding the lives of others lightly in esteem the ancients not unnaturally paid little regard to their own. The responsibility of human life was not realized; men considered their lives absolutely their's and sanctioned suicide.

Centuries of education and experience have stamped their results on our very natures, and by the law of hered-ity we inherit the precious lessons of the past engraven in our very souls. A child of to-day, even without teaching, is more conscientious—*i. e.*, has a better developed conscience than a child of antiquity, because it has the advantage of centuries of experience—just as its mind is naturally more expanded, because the mind of all the human race has been registering thought for ages and ages, until the brain, marvelous always, has still more marvellously unfolded its glories.

I have said that conscience is a power of our reason and gives knowledge of morals. But conscience is not confined to our cognitive powers. But in directing the reason to distinguish between right and wrong conscience necessarily invades also the realm of feeling. For mind has three phases—knowing, feeling, willing. Nearly every experience is accompanied by a feeling either of pleasure or pain. Great part of our life is spent in avoiding pain and seeking pleasure. I may say this gives the motive to all action. When conscience points out moral law to the human being, the feeling of pleasure or pain assists it, obedience being accompanied by pleasure, disregard by pain. Feeling as well as reason can be educated. The more faithfully we obey the dictates of conscience the more sensitive do our feelings become to the finer shades of right and wrong; and when a nature in which the moral is highly developed disobeys the inward monitor, the sensation of pain is positively distressing. This pain after the deed is called remorse. Thus the very suffering helps us toward the right. The knowledge of duty seems then to come through feeling, or more exactly the knowledge comes first and the feeling follows instantaneously. A child wishes to take what is not his. Immediately conscience telegraphs from brain that this is wrong, then a disagreeable sensation that is half dread and half shame fills the being, and the object is dropped because the sin seems to bring more suffering than possession would bring joy.

This, however, is not always the conclusion. If the forbidden object be very much coveted, or conscience be not well educated, the moral warning will be crushed and the desire fulfilled. We are creatures of habit, and if the still small voice be disregarded a few times, it soon ceases to trouble us. That is the dangerous period of life, when not conscience but simply policy keeps us from complete ruin, when we fear not sin but discovery, when we are appalled not by guilt but by failure.

The words "moral" and "custom" come from the same root. For moral is supposed to make custom, and this was the original idea. The realization of innate modesty, of the rights of possession, of the sanctity of life, created the customs of protecting chastity, property and life, and of punishing those who violated them. But at times we pervert the normal purpose in the misdirection of our conscience, and instead of an act becoming customary because it is right, it is made right because it has become customary. "For use almost can change the stamp of nature."

Habit will enable us so to adjust convenience and duty that we can even succeed in deceiving ourselves. The Caffers have practised sheep-lifting so long that it is dignified into a national custom. Perhaps the person who lives by petty thieving gets so used to it as eventually to regard it as a trade, and to speak of it as one would speak of any regular business. Think of the innocent coast villagers in the last century who would complacently put up false lights so that a ship might be wrecked on the coasts and then plunder the booty from the bodies washed ashore in the morning!

War is such a universal institution that no country seems to have any conscientious scruples about it. Custom has made it seem right. Therefore we look with pride on our great warriors, hold them up as examples to our children and preserve their forms in conspicuous places in bronze, marble and granite. And indeed conditions have made them worthy of this esteem. For custom has led man to resort to war to wipe out injustice and to further noble aims. And yet I am convinced that a later and a better age will class war with human sacrifice and religious massacres.

"Misery loves company," says a proverb, so does sin. Nay, "company" seems to remove the stigma of sin. Give plenty with us and we will do anything. For when others side with an individual—he is said to have "moral support." I think the kenest prohibition in the Mosaic Law is: "Go not after the multitude to do evil." A safer maxim than *vox populi vox dei.*

Fifty years ago very few Jews broke the Sabbath. Walking through the Jewish quarter one saw nearly all the shutters up. When one or two then decided to do business on that day they felt conscience-stricken and ashamed. They would go down-town stealthily, or perhaps they would open only a side-door. But now, nearly everybody breaks the Sabbath. Therefore, the shame seems to be removed. Custom has made it a matter of course. And if one happens to be found here and there, who does keep the Sabbath, people express surprise. Even the minister can no longer demand Sabbath observance—that stage has passed. It has actually ceased to be regarded as duty.

Custom and the majority will condone the evasion of revenue duties and income-taxes, the deceptions and misrepresentations of 'business," the adulteration of products, the "white lies" and fox-hunting of polite society.

Indeed, we defend so much that is indefensible if it contributes to our pleasure. Birds are robbed of their feathers while alive to contribute to the vanity of women.

To make it more inviting, cod is "crimped"—that is, cast alive in boiling water; this same treatment gives redness to the lobster.

Most people accept things as they find them, taking refuge in authority and precedents. If an abuse exists that does not trouble them, although they feel it wrong they let it be—simply saying—"Things are that way, you know—were so before I came; it is no business of mine to alter; I would create unpleasantness; get myself disliked, and still perhaps accomplish nothing."

Custom is a labor-saving-machine; it saves thought and makes action automatic. "That monster custom, who all sense doth eat of habits evil, is angel yet in this, that to the use of actions fair and good he likewise gives a frock or livery that aptly is put on." It is always easier for a cart to travel in the ruts made by the wagons that preceded it. It is always easier, safer and less responsible to follow than to lead.

At the time that some of our municipal institutions were being overhauled—the chief defense for corrupt practices, was that everybody did it, it was the usual thing. So everywhere custom and the majority seem to make moral. It even permits respectable young men to lead immoral lives and still be considered respectable and worthy. Such are the customs of modern society. If unchastity is not absolutely defended, it is at least connived at when the young men do not go too far; they are told by their friends—not, to be virtuous, but to be prudent.

Custom adjusts conscience, to look with complacency even on our weaknesses. Whatever conventionality defends we are satisfied to do. Young ladies are more anxious to do the "correct" thing than the right thing. Mark the distinction. The behests of Mrs. Grundy are more vigorously followed than Moses and the prophets.

Thus conscience like reason, like every one of our senses, can be cultivated on the lines of perfection or can be distorted out of all recognition of itself. Fidelity to its behests even under great temptations will reward its owner by refining every sensibility and trait until he become indeed one of nature's gentlemen, one of God's noblemen; like Washington he will be unable to lie, like a well-known Roman he will love honor more than life, like Aristides, justice will become one of his names.

Disregard of the warnings of conscience will so degrade the whole nature, check its worthy impulse, and deaden all nobler feeling that in the abandoned creature left, no trace will be there to show the image of God; like Attila he will earn the title of Scourge of God, like Nero he will burn a city to see a blaze, like the Australian savage he will dash a child to pieces in a fit of anger.

We are gifted with conscience, we are also gifted with free-will. We are not automata moved in certain lines by unknown hands; we are independent creatures given liberty of action. Our destiny is in our own hands; we can raise ourselves to godliness, or sink ourselves to beastliness.

The soil of our soul is given to each to tend. He may allow the ill-weeds of sin that grow so apace to choke it, or he may plant it with rare virtues, the flowers of character, until the soul becomes indeed like a "garden that the Lord hath planted."

THE IMMORTALITY OF THE SOUL

I.

The doctrine of Immortality concerns us almost as profoundly as the doctrine of God. Our happiness in this life depends more than we suppose on what our belief of the hereafter may be. If we think that death means extinction, our conception of life, of its purpose and its good, will be very different from what it would be if we believed that death was but a change preparatory to entering a higher state of being. I therefore consider it an all-important theme for religious treatment and religious contemplation.

There is such a mistaken opinion as to the place of futurity in Judaism that I had better begin by telling its attitude both in antiquity and in modern days. The absence of distinct mention of the future life in the Mosaic Law has led some to suppose that this doctrine was not then believed. For that matter silence may mean two things, either absolute unbelief or absolute acceptance beyond all question. As a matter of fact, complete, utter extinction was never a belief of the Hebrews even of the earliest times. The departed all went to Sheol which from its state of passivity was not so much unlike some conventional pictures of heaven. It corresponded most closely to the classical Hades. But just as the Bible presents to us growth in the idea of God, in the standard of morals and in all human obligation, so we find a growth in this doctrine too. We see the shadowy Sheol deepen into Immortality. The theology of the later Psalms is very different from that of the earlier ones. In that wonderful spiritual advance that characterized the Exile we find a more explicit statement of this great hope. The later prophets were no longer satisfied with the theory of nationalism, viz., that the individual was sacrificed or ignored, and only the fate and future of the people as a whole considered· They began to teach the theory of individualism : "the soul that sinneth it shall die," and the soul that conquereth sin shall live.

Some of the later Bible quotations that suggest this belief with more or less distinctness are these :

" I have set before thee life and death, blessing and curse, therefore choose life that thou mayest live, thou and thy seed." (Deut. xxx., 19.)

"I said I have labored in vain, I have spent my strength in naught and vanity, yet surely my judgment is with the Lord, my recompense is with God." (Is. xlix., 11.)

" Thy dead shall live : thy dead bodies shall arise· Awake and sing ye that dwell in the dust, for the earth shall cast forth the dead." (Is. xxvi., 19.)

"Thou wilt not leave my soul in Sheol, neither wilt thou suffer thy pious one to see corruption; thou wilt show me the path of life." (Ps. xvi., 10.)

" I shall be satisfied when I awake with thy likeness." (Ps. xvii., 15.)

" But God will redeem my soul from the power of Sheol." (Ps. xlix., 15.)

Here is a quotation from the Book of Daniel, which, being one of the latest books introduced into the Bible, presents this doctrine in its fullest development :

"And many of them that sleep in the dust of the earth shall awake, some to everlasting life, some to everlasting contempt. They that be wise shall shine as the bright-ness of the firmament, and they that turn many to right-eousness as the stars for ever and for ever." (Daniel xii., 2.)

External conditions all now tended to strengthen the

belief in futurity in the Israel of the Second Kingdom.
The fall of colossal empires opened to their contemplation the vastness of history and the sublime immensity
of the world. The influence of Persian ideas told upon
them too. Under the persecutions of Antiochus Epiphanes they saw their fairest and noblest die the martyr's
death—was that to be the end of them? Surely not, if
God is just. That martyrdom, therefore, produced the
Book of Daniel as well as the Feast of Chanuka. The
hope of the future life, its rewards and its punishments
are here distinctly stated. Indeed the main purpose of
the book was to encourage the down-hearted in that
terrible period of "storm and stress," and to assure
them that God's justice and love never failed, but
extended even beyond the grave. This book was the
forerunner of a whole department of literature—apo-
cryphal and apocalyptic, that expanded with growing
fervor this now all-absorbing belief. Even the Messianic hope came to be associated with the Resurrection.
And none taught and believed in futurity so intensely
as the often despised Pharisees.

I could spend a long time in giving you quotations
from the Rabbinical writings that express their convictions of the life beyond the grave, such as "The righteous
of all faiths shall inherit future bliss," or " this world is
a vestibule, the next world is a palace," their calling the
cemetery חיים בית—House of Life—and their speculations
about Ge-Hinnom and Paradise. But I will pause only
to point out a distinction between the Christian and the
Jewish conception of futurity. Even in the thorniest
days of mediæval Judaism the life beyond the grave was
never permitted to usurp the legitimate joys or boundless
opportunities of the life this side of it. Unlike the
Christian, they never called this world "a vale of tears"
hough they had perhaps more justification for doing so

Without actually saying so, they considered it an accusation against God and an aspersion on this life to regard it simply as a disagreeable waiting period of probation. They therefore discouraged asceticism and called it sinful; the Nazarite was the exception that proved the rule. Nor did they think it fair to God or man to regard marriage as a mere concession to human frailty.

In the second place, while believing that the wicked would be punished after death, they never dwelt much on that side of immortality, but laid larger stress on its hopeful view—and they certainly never carried this punishment of the wicked to the development of a doctrine of "everlasting punishment." Those Jews that have come to believe in hell at all, have picked it up from Christianity. So to-day in modifying our belief in the future to a scientific foundation, dropping the belief in the resurrection of the body and expanding the belief in the immortality of the soul, we, unlike the Universalists and Unitarians, have not found it necessary to officially renounce our belief in everlasting punishment since we have never consciously accepted it. In other words Judaism has never attempted to put in specific pictures its conceptions of rewards and punishments in the after-life—has felt satisfied in declaring its belief in the future as such, but considered it derogatory and irreverential to give serious form to the fancies of the imagination as to what that future may be. May not this be akin to that characteristic aversion of the Jew to make an image of God?

Not giving then to the doctrine as a whole the prominence in our theology or life that Christianity gives to it, and being silent altogether about hell-fire, purgatory and the devil, added to the absence of this doctrine from the Mosaic Law—have led some people actually to suppose that we did not hold this doctrine at all. And even some Jews, with that habit of theirs of letting Christians tell them what Judaism is, have supposed this too—forgetting that Resurrection is the subject of the thirteenth creed of Maimonides—the only attempted formulation of Jewish doctrine in all our history.

So much for the official doctrine within Judaism and for its ecclesiastical authorization. But, as in all other cardinal doctrines, the world to-day has not been satisfied with the authority of what we call revelation, with the teachings of the Scriptures and the past, but also needs a rational demonstration that will appeal to their own reason and emotion, it is asking on what ground outside of ecclesiastical authority do we maintain this belief to-day. It is of the proofs, analogies and suggestions of this character that we will now treat. But in attempting to demonstrate immortality from Natural Religion as distinct from Revealed as in the attempt to demonstrate God--absolute proof for both is beyond us. Our belief in God and in our future state must ultimately rest on faith, and it is well perhaps that they should. But faith is often fed and fostered by reason. I am going to show you the reasonableness of immortality.

Belief in the immortality of the soul must first be preceded by a belief in the soul itself. There is a class of thinkers who deny the existence of what we call the soul—that is, they deny that it is anything different in kind from the body, that like the body it is but matter, that all our sensibilities, emotions, feelings and thoughts are but emanations of matter in more or less refined degrees, varying chiefly in velocity of movement—reminding us of the ancient atomic theory. In brief, that there is nothing in the universe inside of man or outside but matter. These are materialists. To them naturally the dissolution of the body is the dissolution of the individual.

If we do not want to be taken too far away from our theme, we might show how a philosophy of materialism explains away even conscience, by making it the result of experience ; explains away merit or blame and hence morality by making them as purely the consequences of physical conditions as diseases and health, and finally explains away freedom of will. You see how all religion and how all that is highest and noblest in life is indirectly connected with the belief in immortality, and directly connected with the beliefs that support that belief.

We find ourselves possessing a body, and through some of its organs we experience certain sensations. We find that thought leaves a physical impress in a portion of the body called the brain, and that every emotion is accompanied by some physical indication. And when the heart—the centre of the physical system—stops beating, life ceases and the body decays and crumbles into dust. Now is this body with its complicated apparatus, its muscles, its nerves and its blood, all that there is of us? Do certain secretions bring thought and certain movements love; or are these secretions and movements of matter merely their physical accompaniments?

This question we can partly answer. It has been scientifically demonstrated that, come our thoughts and emotions whence they may, matter is not their cause. That degree of materialism is already exploded. Furthermore, analogies and comparisons rather favor the view that the individual is behind the body, so to speak, using it as man uses and directs his tools to carry out his purposes. Man invents a telescope that increases the intensity of his own eye and gives it new powers,—an added eye, so to speak; but, however closely he may copy the mechanism, he can never make an eye that will see if the sight of his eye has gone. Does he really see with the eye of flesh, or is the optic power in the individual, though needing certain physical conditions in the eye to exercise it ? Closing the eye altogether, cannot his mind call up actual pictures of things ? In dream he goes through all sensations witout the use of the senses A swoon shows the suspension of many powers and yet they are all there. An anæsthetic will take away the senses, but they return again.

Again, like Laura Bridgeman, an individual may be deprived of many senses, even at birth—of hearing (and therefore of speech), of sight and of taste—and yet the mind. lacking these all-important bodily equipments by which man is enabled to communicate with the outer world, deprived of these prime sources of education, can attain its full vigor, with all its thinking capacity. Laura Bridgeman became a head-teacher in a deaf and dumb school. We can also dispense with many limbs and organs. All these instances merely tend to show the complete dependence of body on mind, and the partial independence of mind.

The fact most inexplicable from the materialistic stand-point is self-conscious personality. I do not know if you ever paused to think all that it means, spiritually speaking, to say the word—I—to realize yourself as an individual. Think of this remarkable preservation of our own identity in all life's changes from youth to old age. Although the body is in a constant flux, falling away and being recreated from material from without, although even the mind undergoes modification and expansion, we never lose trace of ourselves. There we are at the foreground of our being from the beginning to the end. Is this self-conscious, persistent personality a modicum of matter, delicately, subtly arranged, so that it can merge into thought—give itself a name, decide to become moral ? On the contrary we could more easily imagine a condition of pure reflection doing without a body. Some philosophers even doubt the actuality of *matter* and call it but an impression of mind.

At times it seems to us that the body even hampered, stood in the way of our highest and purest conceptions of things. The body imprisoning the soul is more than poe ic trope. It has seemed to many that the fleshy tenement debased the mind to the carnal; we not infrequently speak of the body–"the flesh" contemptuously —the unworthy part of us. Only because it is so indissolubly associated with us. is it hard for us to imagine any kind of life without it, in spite of life's constant experience of the dispensability of the presumed indispensable. In spite of ourselves, the tangible largely affects us and must. We talk of spirit, but we do not know what it is. So that the denial of futurity would be the more obvious supposition, just as a visible divinity first appealed to man rather than an invisible. Not to be seen was not to be.

And yet, if we have learnt anything from the ages, it is that "things are seldom what they seem," that the unseen forces are the greatest forces. The human being, bodily speaking, is almost the same in death as in life— there are all the organs intact, there is the machinery ready to be wound up; but there is an intangible, invisible unknown something absent that makes us call that which lies before us no longer a person, but merely clay to be cast with other clay. The matter is all there. But the matter is the least of the man.

Not knowing what life is, of course, we do not know what death is, we only know some of its effects. It removes from view; it destroys a sensible proof of existence. We see even in lower visible nature certain forms of death that are really entrances in higher forms of life. We see worms creep into the darkness, weave their own coffins from which they burst into higher life with new kinds of needs. So mysteriously wonderful is the implanted instinct that I read recently when the lava of the male stag-beetle becomes a chrysalis it builds its nest larger than itself because in its new existence it will have horns. Do caterpillars ever speculate of their after-life as butterflies, I wonder? We see a tree each winter reduced to a skeleton, robbed of its product and its beauty, standing gaunt against the winter skies as though awaiting burial—we see new life and new beauty and new fruits burst all over it again, and the annual resurrection is sometimes repeated for hundreds of years. We are told that matter lives for ever, taking different forms. We are told that forces persist through all time and never die into nothing. Only the continuity of the human being, the master-piece of God, is doubted.

Can we sit down calmly and believe that we are each in turn to pass away into non-existence after this short struggle, that we call life, is over and never to know what it all means, creation, development, morals, suffering, aspiration, God? Is humanity but an incident in an endless series of cosmical changes, with their final outlook annihilation?

TEMPLE ISRAEL PULPIT.

SERMONS OF DR. M. H. HARRIS.

Published Weekly at 213-215 East 44th Street, New York.

VOL. II. NO. 4.   FEBRUARY 22 1895.   *Subscription One Dollar.*

IMMORTALITY.

II.

So many new experiences in the unseen world of spirit that we thought beyond human possibility have come to us in the last few years, that we have to revise our conclusions about the limits of human knowledge. We are already talking of a sixth sense, and taking fully into account all the delusions and frauds of spiritualism and clairvoyance—there is a residuum of demonstrated data as to mind communion and mind influence at a distance, that has received the name of telepathy, and also some remarkable experiments in hypnotism and animal magnetism that suggest, if nothing more, at least vast and unsuspected powers of soul, unaided by and apart from the body. We are at the present moment on the eve of expectancy of the new world that these researches may open up to us. Many men whose mental vigor is as unquestioned as their sincerity, and who hesitate to accept even that which is fully proven, are beginning to recognize that there are capacities in our spirit-nature that cannot be ignored. We have almost exhausted the possibilities of matter, we have hardly tried the potentialities of spirit. And while these conclusions may not directly touch the question of the soul's immortality, they do indirectly bear upon it, by teaching that human life means a good deal more than we popularly suppose. They help us to realize at least that we cannot in the course of one life bring out all the capacities of our being. I am not now speaking of the young man, who having devoted all his years to education, for the mere preparation of life, is suddenly cut off before that life in its actual reality begins I am confining myself now to those who reach the fifty or sixty years that comprise the average earthly career. We grow old before we know what life means. We feel certain stirrings within us that never come to maturity, but which dimly teach how little we know the magnitude of our own selves. For a moment, certain depths of our nature are opened up and we catch a glimpse of our more exalted self. It soon shuts down and we turn to our grubbing existence of externals and things, which is but mere playing on the outside of life; then comes death after we have had but a few hints of being. The physician does not yet know the use of the pineal gland and the tonsils; but think of the many emotions, yearnings and aspirations whose functions we have failed to unravel. We speak of reaching maturity—no life reaches maturity—no life is fully ripened. In nature we see the blossom die that the fruit may come. "All flesh is grass," says the prophet, yes we only reach the blossom stage! For moral perfection is the fruit and maturity of the soul. No life is long enough to carry out its own plans, not to speak for a moment of attaining to its ideals. Many a human work —a great cathedral—takes the years of many lives to complete. Why should a star live longer than fifty generations of men? There is nothing more incomplete than the most complete of human lives. When we think that every one of us have in a more or less developed condition the powers of the artist, the prophet, the inventor, the poet, the hero, the philosopher—that we might each one of us be all of these, and that no one ever attains in a great degree to more than one or at the most

to two of these powers, while the vast majority reach no
further than the germ condition, we can form some idea
of the fragmentary character of life.   If we are given
powers that range through all time, should our lot be
that of "the beasts that perish?"

We find certain infinities in ourselves although we call
ourselves finite.   In the first place our mind has been
able to imagine infinity—by conceiving the word.   We
find in ourselves the power for endless growth and improvement intellectually and spiritually.   Our conception of vastness in time and space, and power, and knowing, and being, makes this life insufficient for our aspiring
nature.   It breaks through the earthly bonds that hold
it back from entering on its eternal residence.   Like
Moses it sees the Promised Land but cannot reach it.
The more we advance the nobler the soul expands, the
more intensely our conscious personal individuality is
developed, the deeper our sense of vitality grows,—the
more difficult does it become to imagine its extinction.
If we are pessimists and think cheaply of life, we may
be glad when it is over and neither desire nor believe its
continuance.   But if life to us is a grand, noble, glorious
gift, if we are inspired by its sublimity, then do we cling
to the necessity of its eternity.

There does not seem in one short life, scope enough
for the demonstration of the divine purpose for humanity.
Our life seems to be built on a large plan of long continuance.   Our very aspirations hint at higher realms of
purer and loftier human activity.   Notice how different
man is from the brute creation; he is not satisfied merely
to fulfil his material wants—the needs and pleasures of
physical existence.   Oh no! he must know everything
and must be everything.   This never-ending emulation
of man has been put in many forms of poetry and fable—
one is, that Prometheus climbed to the heavens and stole

the fire of the gods, and this Titanic spark, placed in the breast of humanity spurred him on to endless triumph. Voluntarily man gives up the conditions of ease and secure existence, and taking his life in his hand goes forth to subdue the world, to wrest its secrets and to fathom the unfathomable. He gives himself to causes whose issue cannot come till long after his present life· He commences great works that he knows he cannot finish. He will not rest until he finds out the nature of himself, the nature of God, the causes of all effects and the effects of all causes. Why is this longing to penetrate the beyond given us, if we cannot penetrate the beyond, if it is ever to elude us and if we are to pass away, never knowing the mystery of our own being or the riddle of the universe? Our yearnings go beyond our faculties, our faculties are superior to our condition·

It is scientifically stated that "every organic instinct has its correlate"—*i. e.*, wherever we find a persistent and vital need in nature we nearly always find the means of its gratification. So far is this true that the existence of a need is almost the indication of the existence of that which will satisfy it. "There is no fundamental expectation of body or soul that has not its probable fulfilment." Because we feel thirst, we know there must be water. The moral necessity that nearly all humanity feels for the existence of God is one of our most convincing proofs of His existence. We find the need and hence the belief of God among people of all religions, however divergent their ethics and observances. The longing for immortality is almost as general. It is part of that "self-preservation" which is "Nature's first law." It is hard for any individual to reconcile himself to extinction—to realize that at the end of this life he will be nothing—will pass right out of existence as though he had never been· The fact that so many of us feel an all-devouring desire to continue being, the fact that this is the sustaining pillar in many lives—may not unreasonably lead us to infer that this instinct has not been put within us to deceive us with a false hope.

"Whence this secret dread and inward horror of falling into nought? Why shrinks the soul back on herself and startles at destruction? 'Tis the divinity that stirs within us. 'Tis heaven itself that points out a hereafter, and intimates Eternity to man."

Another great need of the soul is that attaining of absolute justice that we do not know in this life. We get a rough approximation of justice at best. Chance and accident are important factors in existence. The world's prizes seldom go to the best nor are misfortune and failure by any means the lot of the worst. Prudence is a safer condition of success than nobility. The honors and the blessings are very unequally distributed. As Job puts it : "One man full of blessings dieth in quietness and peace, another dies in bitterness of soul, having never tasted good." There is so much unfairness that we would like to see adjusted and that our inherent sense of right tells us should be, will be. For our human longing for good, for the reign of righteousness is, next to life, humanity's most persistent instinct. Both then intellectually and morally we have a sense of incompleteness, as though we only see half the picture and hence its appearance of want of harmony. We find that tribulation is a condition of existence, yet we do not know why it should be so. We suffer and deny ourselves; there is much pain in our inheritance, but we are buoyed up with the thought that it will all be righted. For otherwise how can we explain to ourselves the purpose of life and its hardships, the woes and the throes that come to every child of man ? Extinction defeats the purpose of moral improvement. People often grow more considerate and more spiritual in advancing years, when on the very brink of the grave. Is all that moral growth to end there?

In answer to such question there is a worthy sentiment of which George Eliot's "Let me join the choir invisible" is the most popular expression, that the nobility we develop is inspiring example to others, and that in this way we, as it were, live in others, and perpetuate the good. But granted that a fraction of the good emanating from a few rare souls may exercise a passing influence on some others—which is after all but a brand plucked from the burning—if oblivion is to overtake them too, and extinction to be the fate of humanity, what then? There is something very mournful and stoical about the goodness of the agnostic—as though it would say, "we are all in this same boat of misery—let us make it as pleasant for each other as possible till we all go out in the darkness. Make shift as best you can —it will soon be over." For according to the received scientific conclusions, all life will, in the "process of the suns," die off from this planet and it will, become like the moon; the sun will cool down into a dying fire and then all these planets will roll into their respective suns, a nebulous cloud of fire will be formed like that at the beginning, and evolution begin its round once more.

What purpose would be attained by all the ages of human development if, after the death of the body, the soul were not to rise into a higher existence, independent of the growth and fall of planets? What would be the ultimate object of human life if, in process of epochs, having at last reached the climax of civilization, the highest pinnacle of thought, the topmost rung in spiritual acquisition—if, after millenia and millenia of human conflict and anguish and consuming effort, all concentrated, let us say, in the last generation—that ultimately the whole temple of our humanity is to be overthrown, cast into the waste-heap of defunct planets, to evaporate in smoke from a monstrous conflagration?

Surely humanity is not a grotesque fancy—a whim of divinity. We get glimpses of good purpose in it all; we see fragments of vast designs. We notice an unbroken upward growth, of which we are part, and to which we are made to contribute. On the belief that it will all be conserved, made to feed a higher and more intense life, does the wisdom and love of God best manifest itself. Even the sacrifices, the struggles, the pains, on the theory of an after-life, become but temporary evil for larger and lasting good. All the ills of humanity fall into their place, helping the everlasting cause: Then the poet's lines come back to us with encouraging promise :

> Oh, yet we trust that somehow good
> Will be the final goal of ill
> To pangs of nature, sins of will,
> Defects of doubt and taints of blood.
> That nothing walks with aimless feet,
> That no one life shall be destroyed
> Or cast as rubbish to the void
> When God hath made the pile complete.

When we think of life as a school of discipline for a grander and ultimate existence, its greatness is magnified, for that which may be noble as subordinate is poor if it is the whole. It is helpful, indeed, to think that our experience has an eternal quality, that every tear and throb goes but to the enrichment of a soul that will blossom for all time. Our very failures, our dissatisfaction, the inequalities that we chafe against, are made part of our earthly education. The fewer ideals we attain, the more there is to work for, the more do we realize the necessity of farther-reaching opportunity. And those whom we call the wicked—the unfortunates, the world's outcasts, humanity's offscourings—it would seem that they more than the righteous would in all fairness need another chance. Having groped through a degraded existence of sin and misery, should that be all of life that exists for them ? Does not our very belief in God's justice demand that opportunity should be given them to redeem the sad and wicked past ?

Even death, on the theory of immortality, has its grateful purpose. We tire after a few years; the earthly frame is only constructed to run for about half or three-quarters of a century. We need the death-sleep, so that we may awaken again with renewed youth and fresh experience. Perhaps there may be a series of deaths between a long series of lives, each stage a higher than the preceding,

We do not know. The conviction must ultimately be an act of faith. We are almost glad of the uncertainty. What sweet elements in life would be lost if certainty came to remove hope and trust! We all agree with Lessing—rather search for the truth than to know it all at once. We do not even wish to have the veil lifted from the next year of this life, preferring to remain in the grateful obscurity, and waiting with pleased expectancy the unfolding of each new day.

So our conclusions as to what our future life may be, are wholly of conjecture. If it is to be a heaven that will invite the longings of man, then it must not be a place of idleness nor even of perfect serenity; we would not wish all the conflicts over and all the battles won, for unless we are to be very differently constituted, we would desire no life without effort, or even without pain of some kind. We would wish to be perpetually growing in all noble directions, bringing out our human possibilities, expanding in realms that have no cramping limitations. We would then desire the future life to be as Tennyson has expressed it—"the glory of going on and still to be."

I need hardly add in closing, that it can be no future life if our consciousness of our own personal identity does not remain. Indeed, the individual must be even more intensely developed, for this is a phase of advancing life. We go down the scale to an unconscious mechanical life, where the animal merges into the vegetable; we rise in the scale until the revealed inner being is disclosed to the self-realized individual in an intellectual and spiritual magnificence that almost merges into the divine. Self-realization—the knowing of ourselves, the unfolding of our complete identity, is our highest attainment, inseparable from all our varied growth When that is taken, all is taken. Unconsciousness is death, identity is life.

WHAT IS THE PURPOSE OF PUBLIC WORSHIP?

It is our duty to take nothing for granted that we can investigate for ourselves. Faith begins only where human research ends. It is our prerogative to examine anew every obligation that comes down to us as an inheritance from the fathers, to add our own convictions to theirs if we can, and thus deepen the sanctity of the principle; or, if need be, to part company with their conclusions and to reach an independent decision. In this way, while we have retained much that is old, we have modified much, and some institutions of the past have in our later wisdom been entirely swept away. While we accept the principle, "Whatever is is right," when applied to the ultimate fact of life, and regard it as the basis of our most inspiring optimism, it is a killing of the spirit of this maxim to quote it in justification for leaving untouched those human institutions that man has made and which, therefore, man can alter.

We hold in our sanctuaries periodic services of prayer and praise and moral instruction. We did not institute these services for ourselves, they were here when we came, we have simply continued them ; and since so much human energy and time and thought and means are expended on these sanctuaries for public worship, it is our right, it is our duty to ask ourselves that great question of the age, *cui bono?* what benefit does public worship render to man ?

Like most human institutions, it has not been deliberately formed. It is a growth. First comes the prophet to teach a new truth. When it is widely accepted, lesser men who lack the genius of prophecy are entrusted with its care—the priests. (Prophets are rare and spoken of

singly with a distinct individuality for each one : priests
are many and are treated collectively, winning authority
by numbers). Gradually an organization grows around
the spiritual truth, periodic observances are instituted for
its regular teaching and confession. The religious
symbols, the doctrinal formulas, the ecclesiastical ceremonial slowly expand in continued elaborateness until
the time arrives when the formalities that were supposed
to embody the great idea begin at last to hamper it or
even to hide it out of sight. Then a reaction takes place
and men ask to go back to first principles, to the old
simple teachings; and a form of worship of barest simplicity is started anew. But in process of time, under
the same inevitable law, certain associations will come
to cluster around that simple service to adorn and enrich
it, that appeal to the imagination and the emotions.

It is not for us to say that any form of worship, however elaborate its ritual or intricate its ceremonial, is
wrong ; or that any worship, however plain its liturgy,
is necessarily the ideal service ; what the ideal shall be
depends in each case upon our different natures. To
some, the sparse ritual of radical denominations consisting chiefly of a sermon with but a prayer, a psalm and a
hymn to lead up to it, and another hymn to round it off
would seem cold and insufficient, while they would welcome the long and varied liturgy of conservatism with
its chanting, its genuflexions, its setting of stained glass,
rich vestments and ponderous architecture, as most satisfying to their religious needs.

I do not wish to consider the nature of the service of
the synagogue now, but only the fact of it. I use the
word " synagogue " advisedly, by the way. It is strange
that our Jewish reformers should have chosen for their
house of worship the name " temple " rather than synagogue, for it is the more orthodox term of the two and

marks an earlier stage in religious development. The "temple" in Judaism, as well as in heathenism, was the place of sacrifice, and all its associations are priestly. The very word "temple" comes from a root that means "to cut," for the Roman augur would cut or rather mark off in his mind's eye a certain portion of the heavens where he would decide to watch the flight of birds, and from their movements foretell a coming event, and so the word "temple" derived from this act shows us where superstition and religion met at one point. "Synagogue" is a Greek word and means a gathering together, corresponding somewhat to "congregation;" it was the place where our ancestors met for prayer at a time when the influence of the temple was beginning to wane, and where the more thoughtful and earnest felt that they could open their hearts to their Father more directly. It was a most vital spiritual advance. And when the temple was destroyed and the institution of sacrifice died out with it, the synagogue remained as the Jewish place of prayer.

——But to return: what is the purpose of the place of worship, call it what you will? Originally it was supposed that the Divine Worship was for the divinity. It was the opportunity for man to fulfil his obligations to his Creator, offering his sacrifices or his prayer in accordance with the injunctions of his faith, acknowledging to God his dependence upon Him, and thanking Him for His blessings. We are satisfied to-day that our public worship is not for God, but for man; that, like religion itself of which it is an expression, it is only for God in the sense we owe it to Him to make the very most of this gift of life and soul that He has bestowed upon us, and that by communion with Him we may be elevated, exalted and purified. This is the ultimate purpose behind all our different religious services, vary as they may. Is

that purpose attained? Are we drawn nearer to God by
offering our prayers to Him? Are we helped to obey the
command by hearing them recited? Are we strengthened
in right by weekly listening to the moral instruction
from the pulpit? Are we inspired by the music and by
the congregational praise? Or, does public worship help
us even in a material way? For, if any souls coming
here from one Sabbath to another Sabbath can feel that
it is indeed a place of rest, and if the worship exercises
upon them a soothing influence only, if it lifts their
burdens for a little time, so that they can go away feeling cheered and encouraged to take up their task once
more,—if the sanctuary served that one purpose only, it
would be a great boon indeed to humanity and would
be worth all the energy and means that it costs to maintain it.

Here and there we by chance find out that this purpose
is rendered. Occasionally the minister is encouraged
by learning that some truth that he had uttered had
gone home, and had been a means of helpfulness and
solace to a fellow-being, and that each time that message
was remembered, it was a new source of comfort and
inspiration. Once in a while, the minister, aiming in
the dark, scattering his seed promiscuously, without
looking, not knowing whom his words may hit, for
whom they may be most helpful—occasionally, I say, a
chance word of his—perhaps not that word that is most
prized by himself—takes root in some desolate heart and
fills it with cheer. yielding a harvest of good as time
rolls on. Sometimes the bread that he wildly casts upon
the waters returns to him after many days, in the assurance that it has nourished many unknown to him, and
whom he may never know.

And even where the influence for good is not felt by
a worshiper or is not known to him, it may nevertheless

be exercised. The psychologists tell us that there are active in the brain two currents of thought—one, conscious, and the other, in the background ; and when occasionally our thoughts go off in a new direction without apparent cause, it is nothing more than the under-current coming to the front. So, in a similar way, much goes on in this complicated physical system of ours unbeknown to ourselves, especially when we are in normal health, and we are sure that the food we take into our body goes through many alimentary processes, until at last it feeds and builds up the wastes of our system and enters into our fibre and blood. Now, it may be that some of the influence exercised by our public worship, unknown even to ourselves, may be like the under-current of thought in the brain, and some day, when we least expect it, it may present itself. Or, like the nourishment within our system, it may work within the recesses of our nature, weaving itself in the web of our conscience, and coming at last to feed and build our moral fibre.

Again, when we scatter seed on the earth, there may be many seeds that remain on the outside ridge, not falling into the cavity prepared for them, and yet a chance wind a little later may blow them into the recesses of the earth, where they may take root and spring up into blossoms one day. And so the subtle influences of the synagogue may rest upon the surface of our nature without being observed by us, but some day a chance circumstance may draw it in and make it part of ourselves.

And yet, taking into consideration the good consciously and unconsciously effected by any of these processes, I do not feel that our public worship fulfils its holy function in anything like the degree it should. I know that many are untouched by it, that the fools

who come to scoff do not remain to pray, and that some
who come to pray may even remain to scoff. I have
abundant evidence that most prayers are voiced laconi-
cally, and that many lessons are uttered to unlistening
ears. I feel that the worship of the temple has fallen to
a formality, and that many have ceased to expect to be,
stirred by it, and hope, at most, to be interested.

Is this entirely the fault of the service? The success
of divine service depends less upon the worship than
upon the worshiper. Some people go to Europe, to the
great cities and the old historic centres, and find their
culture enriched and their mind broadened by the
wonderful things they see—the ruins of ancient civilization, the galleries of art, the quaint towns, and customs of
others lands; and the summer visit becomes for them a
liberal education. There are others again who make the
"grand tour" on the continent and who are in no way
helped by it. If they remember monumental spots at all
or the places remarkable for natural beauty, it is, as an
English humorist has said, simply by the association of
the different things they may have eaten at these places;
as, for instance, "Lake Geneva, oh, that was the place
where we had that lovely soup." It is true of nearly all
things in life that the influence they may have upon us
depends, not so much on the object, as upon ourselves—
whether we go to it in a receptive mood, whether we
bring to it a ready, yearning nature, or, whether we come
cold and empty, standing before it and expecting it to
pour out all its goodness into our souls. According to
the richness of our nature will be the profit we draw
from the treasures given by God and man. In what
spirit do we approach the house of God? When we
enter the theatre, we come in a passive condition. We
take our seat, with a pleased expectancy for the curtain
to rise and watch with a restful satisfaction what is

represented before your eyes. Now, many come to the service in the same passive mood. They lean back upon the cushioned seats and wait for the service to begin. They listen, pleased with the sweet and solemn music, and may be more or less interested in the discourse; and when the service is over, as when the play is over, they rise from their seats and go. This is not the idea of worship, nor is such the mood in which the divine service is likely to be spiritually helpful. We must not expect anything mysterious or supernatural from the service of prayer. Nor should we, to give yet another example, enter it as though it were a clinic of a physician, where a disease is to be cured by an operation and where we wait for the ether to be administered and the poison to be eradicated from our system by the man of science while we are in a state of unconsciousness. We are not an audience on the one hand, in which the minister and choir are the actors; nor are we patients on the other hand, for which they are the physicians. To suppose there is an occult potency in the service in itself is to be enslaved by superstition. *We* are the actors; the reader and choir are not there to pray and sing for us, but to lead us in prayer and song, so the minister can but indicate the right life, he cannot live it for us.

We must go to our public worship full of earnestness, ready to heartily participate in its exercises. We must come filled with the purpose and the spirit that the place implies. We must come, not to listen to prayer reading, but to pray; not to listen to singing, but to sing; not to go to sleep, but to be zealously alert and thrillingly alive.

I must say that I see a compensation in the orthodox service. There, at least, the very nature of the service compels the worshiper to be very active; at every mention of the name of God, he must respond ברוך הוא וברוך שמו:

he must needs be ready with the אמן at the well-known pauses, and on special occasions, as on closing of the Book of the Law, he must utter aloud a distinct formula; at this place he must rise, and at this place step back three paces; at another he must bow, and at another he must strike his breast as an indication of contrition. In many instances his participance is needed to complement the service which would be incomplete and unfinished if he did not perform the parts assigned for him, many of which are now assigned to the choir. Yet, does this mere activity realize the ideal of worship? If the Reform service lacks participance the orthodox service lacks awe. What is awe? Now, if there is any one thing that awe does not mean, it is decorum; the gulf between these two words could hold a universe. A silent and respectful manner is a necessary part of your breeding that you would exercise in all public places, unless you wish to bring upon yourselves unfavorable criticism. It is a lesson that you have learned from the book of etiquette, not from the books of the prophets. Although some are not even decorous, and so forget the awful sanctity of God's house as to spend the hours of worship in trivial gossip. Of such persons or to them I have to say—nothing. Be our service what it may, it must fail unless the worshiper bring with him to the Temple a quickened sense of the solemnity of the place and the purpose, as though he really thought that the spirit of God dwells within these walls, when man comes to worship there.

He must feel that something higher than fear and deeper than reverence steals over him as he enters the holy calm of the Sanctuary and realize with Jacob that "Verily this is the House of God and the gate of heaven."

Much has been written of the efficacy of prayer. Let me say that you have only to realize what prayer is while uttering it, for its efficacy to be abundant and complete. We stand impressed and moved before a piece of marble that was carved a thousand years ago; if we but thought while we prayed, what would be our emotion as we put ourselves in communication with Him who has sat enthroned in the heart of the universe for millions and millions of ages! We *say* God in two languages and in many synonyms a hundred times in every service, do we *think* God once? Realize in your imagination the Eternal Spirit as you open your hearts for prayer, and the mysterious sanctity that must fill your hearts, and the pure elevation that must enter your being in such prayer, is certainly a sufficient answer.

And so I say, that while the failure of the service to reach and to help you may be partly due to its insufficiency, it is largely due to you. You must meet it half way. The current of its effect is not complete until you have put yourselves in response with it; and only when you give forth your vitality to grasp the electric rods is the circuit complete and can the inspiring solemnity of worship surge through your being.

I feel that this is a very profound question, a question that we dare not treat lightly. I do not ask you to be satisfied with whatever form we may give to you; it is your duty not to submit to a service that does not respond to your needs, but to ask for that which will best reach the depths of your emotions. We would lessen the Hebrew and enlarge the amount of the vernacular if you felt that that was the one thing needful to make it really a service for you. We would lessen the length, if you felt that the tension of inspiration could better be preserved within a shorter period We would vary the service in certain portions from week to week. if you felt that the too oft repeated prayers might lose their power since you become unconscious of their beauty by repeti-

tion and get to utter them automatically. The service is
for you and it is for you to ask that it be so changed or
modified as to respond to the yearnings of your soul for
religious life and religions nurture. Anything but an
apathetic indifference as to what we offer you. Anything
but a dull acquiescence, sitting through a liturgy that
is for you a dead formality.

Either this weekly worship of God is a very real thing
or it is a blasphemy, a taking His name in vain. We
have no right to call upon Him perpetually if we do not
feel the call, if we are merely uttering formulas advanced
by others. We can decide by our earnestness, by our zeal,
by our faith, by our conscientious desire for moral improvement whether divine service shall be a reality or a
sham. The very manner in which many come to service,
letting the slightest occurrence decide their presence, or
absence, lounging in as the whim strikes them, must in
itself defeat its profoundly solemn purpose and vulgarize
its sanctity. The attitude of the worshiper can make the
service a sensational entertainment, a dead formality or
a travesty; the attitude of the worshiper can give to service glory and power and vivifying touch—verily the
union of man with God.

KINGDOM OF PRIESTS.

" If ye obey My voice ye shall be unto Me a kingdom of priests and a holy nation." Ex. xix., 5-6.

A kingdom of priests sounds like a contradiction in terms. It is not unlike a kingdom of kings, which, of course, leads to the question who will be the subjects, or of whom will they be kings. A priest was a representative of divinity to the people. If all the people were priests, whom would they represent? He was the intercessor between God and man, the one who revealed the will of God to the people and presented the wishes of the people to God. Whether in early days among idolatrous cults he was supposed to be vested with occult and magical powers that gave him insight into mysteries, so that he could foretell events as a soothsayer, or by frenzied prayers and incantations even avert them—or whether, as in later monotheistic times, he was simply vested with authority of ecclesiastical law, ceremonial observance and ritual formalities—he was in both instances religious representative of the people. When, then, Israel is called to become a kingdom of priests the term must surely be used in a new sense. You will hasten to answer that they were to be religious priests to the world at large, that this verse refers to their mission to mankind. But I hardly think that that idea was fully reached at the time the injunction was voiced. Only late in its religious development did Israel become fully conscious of its mission to the world. I, therefore, think we must accept the word priest here rather in the sense of prophet. Israel was to be, not a nation of priests, but a nation of prophets. Each represents a fundamentally distinct idea in religion. It is with the spirit of the prophet and not the spirit of the priest that we are in sympathy to-day.

The word "priest" has not come down from history with an entirely satisfactory reputation. It brings with it associations of ceremonialism, narrowness, superstition, even of craft, cruelty and selfishness. There is much to be said for and against the priest in religion's history. He certainly helped to build up organized religion and to preserve it, though his defense of the priestly organization, temples, worship, tithes and offerings, was not always in the interests of spirituality and the highest ethics, and at times directly against them. For he would discourage too bold a truth and too outspoken a sincerity. At times he might be guilty of a pious fraud, such as ascribing ecclesiastical laws to Moses in order to win for them authority and obedience, or in rewriting history in the interests of his class, as in the Book of Chronicles. Roughly speaking, he stood for peace and order and simple virtues in barbaric and lawless times. But when the moral standard of one age, let us say, became crystallized in certain observances, the priests would often be the opponents of a higher moral standard, the outgrowth of a better age, since it tended to interfere with usages which they had created and which had become part of their ecclesiastical institution. For instance, there was a time when the introduction of animal sacrifice was a distinct moral advance over a form of worship grosser still. The priests may have opposed the change, but when, finally, animal sacrifice was accepted, they became its best preservers. Later, however, a higher ethical advance, led as always by the prophets, still saw in this cattle slaughter a degraded system not far removed from idolatry. Again the priests fought for an institution that had now become the chief feature of their Temple service, the chief object of the Temple itself, the main source of their revenues, and, as it seemed to them for the moment the very bulwark of their religion. When they finally yielded, as they always had eventually to give way to the best needs of the age—and prayer replaced the sacrifice—they endeavored as far as possible to retain the sacrificial form, inserting the paragraph that demanded the sacrifice, and closing each service with a prayer that some day sacrifice might be restored.

The priest, then, represents conservatism in religion—all that is good in conservatism and all that is bad in it; the conscientious and painstaking preserver of the records and traditions of the past, the not always conscientious enemy of new ideas and new ideals—calling them hard names—labeling them heresy, infidelity and atheism. In his opposition to the prophets, who always represented the progressive spirit and the high-water mark of morals, he has from time to time precipitated the conflict between religion and ethics that always should go hand in hand, each furthering the other's growth. The greatness of the Decalogue lies in its indissolubly uniting religion and ethics.

It was with all the characteristics of the priest, except the name, that led the Rabbins to elaborate the ceremonial law, to hold to every minute command that could be found or implied in the five books of the Pentateuch, to try to hold back by the force of ecclesiastical authority the progress of Judaism to that particular point where it had been stopped in the Talmud, not by a deliberate act of Judaism's teachers, but simply by external and political legislation. In other words: because illiberal governments closed the Jewish schools, there the progress of our religion had to be suddenly cut off short at the point it had reached when the school closed.

The antagonism between priestism and prophetism,

while then bearing different names for different epochs, was but history's proverbial repetition. In the second kingdom it was Sadduceeism against Phariseeism, in the middle ages it was Rabbinism against Karaism, to-day it is Orthodoxy against Reform. For our problem to-day is exactly the same as that which ranged Amos, Hosea, Isaiah, Micah and Jeremiah against the priests and Levites of Beth-El, Samaria and Jerusalem. The priests pleaded for the old rites which had since become wrongs, for the old customs which had since become superstitious, for the old gods which had since become idols. The prophets pleaded for the people as against ecclesiatical despotism, for the living spirit as against the dead letter, for moral ideals that were beyond man in place of ideals which were behind him.

Those full of the priest-spirit to-day are asking us to worship the old simply because it is old, to accept laws on their antiquity instead of on their merit, and to invest with a distinctly religious character observances and usages that have the right to be called religious and Jewish only by their association with Judaism, but which may have been originally borrowed from other nationalities and secular at that. For instance, the Russian Jew holds to his long coat which was not a Jewish costume, but the old garment of the Russian peasants, which he alone has retained after the fashion has changed. If it were not that climate made it impracticable, I am quite sure that the priest or conservative party in Judaism would insist on our removing, our shoes at service, which Oriental custom was borrowed by the Oriental Hebrews. They still insist on the ceremony of חליצה in an age that is no longer polygamic and whose whole purpose disappears in a monogamic society. They still count the Omer though there is no Omer to count, and pray for the schools of Babylon though the schools of Babylon and Babylon itself are no more.

No one would ask us to live in a house without windows, because when Moses taught the Decalogue glass
was not invented. Because in early ages all nations
looked upon others as enemies, communities kept to
themslves, and caste built walls between class and class,
and this exclusiveness was mirrored in all legislation,
Jewish as well as other, is no reason why to-day we
should continue this policy of selfishness which the
world has outgrown. We Jews have no right to be indifferent to the religious welfare of others, we have no
right to pray only for peace to Israel, it is our duty to
pray for the peace of minkind. We have no right to
retain in our Liturgy or to encourage in our intercourse
a veiled contempt for the Gentile, even on the ground of
retaliation, for no moralist has yet been able to make an
equation in which two wrongs were equivalent to one
right. Because woman was treated with scant consideration in Bible times, not by Jews more than by others,
in fact by Jews less than by others, there is no reason
why we shut her out of the privilege of obeying some
religious injunctions now, or ignore her existence in
counting the quorum for service. We do not think of
introducing slavery because in a modified form it is
approved in Exodus, since it would be forbidden by the
laws of the land. But we ought not to maintain any
outgrown institution in our religion until the law of the
land absolutely prohibits it. We should anticipate and
set the moral example for government laws as we have
done in the past.

For all duties our question must not be, is it old—is it
in the Shulchan Aruch, is it approved by the ecclesiastics
—but *is it right?* We must never feel that our religion
is behind the high moral water mark of the age, that,
instead of urging us on to higher ethical standards, it is
holding us back to lower ideals, since outgrown. It

would be a sad confession to make that religion is following in the wake of ethics instead of leading it, taking
possession of each moral ground only after ethics had
deserted it for a loftier plane.

And since this is perhaps the tendency of priestism
as such in all religions, we must rather join the school
of prophets, be a kingdom of prophets rather than a
"kingdom of priests," which I believe to be the spirit of
the text. Let us be a nation of prophets, let each individual feel separately called to testify to the living God
and to make his life a model of conduct and an example
to all. A later incident in the Pentateuch supports this
view. Joshua hastened one day into the presence of
Moses, his master, in much consternation—two young
men, Eldad and Medad had presumed to act as prophets
among the people, surely a prerogative reserved only for
the great lawergiver himself, but this meekest of men
והאיש משה ענו מאד, with that wonderful spirit of self-abne-
gation that in my opinion is his supreme quality, smiling
indulgently, as we can imagine, on the impetuous Joshua,
sweetly replied: "Art thou jealous for my sake, would
that all the Lord's people were prophets, that the spirit
of God were upon them."

The priests, belonging to one family or one tribe, hand-
ing down their hierarchal or priestly privileges by law
of family descent, maintaining a strict caste and forming
an exclusive aristocracy, stand in striking contrast to
the broad democracy of our text, that would make every
man a minister of God—a whole kingdom of priests—
not a privileged few. And it may have been conscious
or unconscious observance of the spirit of our text that
led the masses of Judeans in the time of the Second
Temple to rebel against the exclusive religious prerogative of the priestly order, and to declare henceforth that
every man should have the right to perform his own

sacrifice, to pray his own prayer, to open his heart direct
to his God, without the meddlesome and not always
worthy intervention of a royal priesthood. Hence the
Pharisees, who ought not to have been called "Separa-
tists," which the name implies; with more fairness that
term should have been applied to the small minority—
the Sadducees--the self-styled elect, above the common
herd, alone fit, in their opinion, to administer the affairs
of religion. When the Jew to-day speeds the departing
Sabbath with a wine and incense offering, he does not
know perhaps that he is carrying out the protest of the
Pharisees of 2,000 years ago, who maintained that every
man could be his own priest and fulfil for himself these
priestly functions ·

The prophet belonged necessarily to no school or
class. He might be a ploughman like Elisha, a gatherer
of sycamore fruit like Amos, a son of the people like
Micah, or on the other hand a man from the aristocracy
like Isaiah. As long as he felt the spirit of God within
him urging him to strike a blow for the oppressed or to
make a great appeal for righteousness, his calling or
condition mattered not. He was self-appointed and his
zeal, sincerity and moral courage were his only pass-
ports or diplomas. He cared not for ancient precedents,
for time-honored usages, for royal· classes or priestly
classes—he cared not even for the established institutions
of religion, if their formal observance stood in the way
of soul-purity and higher duty. So Isaiah hesitated not
to speak with indifference of Sabbaths, New Moons,
Festivals and Divine worship when the elementary virtues were ignored. Jeremiah found it necessary to warn
his people of the insufficiency of the Temple, the very
foundation of priestly importance and power. Of course
they were called traitors, heretics, unbelievers, perhaps
atheists, for their daring defiance of the old prejudices ·

and the old superstitions. But they were not afraid of
hard names and hard blows, of ridicule, of social ostracism, of imprisonment or contumely. All of these were
meted out to them with no reluctant hand.

Now I have always been a great pleader for the retention of the sentimental associations of our religion, of
giving due reverence and regard to the sanctions of
time, and have tried to show that we can advance by
upbuilding, modifying and expanding better than by
overthrowing and destroying. Furthermore, I have
always spoken with distrust of those impulsive spirits,
who, taking up the cry of progress, would with vandal-
hand tear down the monuments of the past that educate
our dignity and feed our inspiration.

The message came to Jeremiah "to root up and tear
down, to build and to plant." There are times when
duty says take up the axe, there are times when she bids
us take in hand the trowel. Your conscientious judgment will seldom lead you wrong as to which is the
nearer need. The harder path is usually the right path.
When it needs heroism to be liberal, then is it duty to
be liberal. When the prophets preached their lofty
morals and advocated sweeping changes they were
speaking against the spirit of the age, and far in advance
of it. So, what might be original and heroic then, might
be commonplace and time-serving now !

But, be the age liberal or conservative, we dare not ever
connive at that which is not quite right, even though our
aim may be an amiable one. Religion must know no
compromise, it dare not juggle with the truth, with the
absolute and highest right. No devotion to sacred
institutions dare blind us to their defects, to their insufficiency for our own times, to the falling off in the
slightest degree from the best that our souls can con-
ceive. Let us be priests in the good sense: lovingly to

preserve the old when it reveals a deep and lasting truth and when it is inspiringly helpful. Let us be prophets in the good sense: to be among the first to hail the new truth and the latest duty. Let us be teachers of the old paths and torch-bearers of the new. Be you then on the alert, see that you not only live up to your religion, but that your religion lives up to you, that its ideals advance with you, that it adjust itself to the noblest thought of every age, that it stand ever in the van-guard of civiliza-tion inviting man with its beckoning promise to come up higher.

JEWISH OSTRACISM.

We Jews can never quite forget our anomalous position in the world. Even if we would forget it, it is con-
stantly brought home to us by external antagonism. In
spite of the great progress that has been made by modern
nations in the idea of freedom, the last stage of freedom
has yet to be attained, that is, liberty to be in the minority,
liberty to deviate from the popular route, liberty to be
different, either in dress, in action, or in ideas. The man
who diverges from prescribed custom is called eccen-
tric and is made uncomfortable in some way; for custom
makes law and sometimes it makes right; to be moral
often means no more than to be conventional. The Jews
of to-day in all countries of the world, though they
represent a very small body, venture to differ from the
religions of their respective neighbors, and stand apart
in their conception of divinity and consequently in their
Weltanschauung. This difference, with the observances
that have grown out of it, has modified their life and
developed distinct characteristics. And, because minorities always expose themselves to persecution, since the
world chafes at exceptions, therefore, the history of the
Jew has largely been a history of persecution.

The Jew has stood aloof from the people about him
almost from the time he first appeared upon the stage of
history. When the Canaanites were his neighbors, he
withdrew from the Canaanites, not perhaps to the extent
that tradition intimates, but yet a withdrawal always
seemed to be the religious ideal in the minds of the earliest
leaders. It was always felt that they were different and
distinct from their surroundings, and that part of the
purpose of their life could only be fulfilled by separa▾

tion; that a commingling with their neighbors would
imply and lead to the surrender of their ideas. A nationality of their own assisted in developing this separation.
And even later, when the Babylonians were their masters,
they did not yield up their individuality to the Babylo-
nian conception of things. When they were the subjects
of the Greek-Syrian rule, they were never identified
either as Syrians or as Greeks, though they imbibed
many Greek ideas; they lived their separate life. The
Romans could never assimilate them, the Mohammedans could never assimilate them, nor could the Christian nations of Europe assimilate them. And because
they were few and because they were different, each of
these nations respectively persecuted them after their
kind.

History even takes their first persecution back as early
as the days of Egypt, fifteen hundred years before the
common era; and the reason which we read between the
lines of the ostensible excuse is that they preserved their
distinct identity. The festival of Chanukah but commemorates their deliverance from religious intolerance
while under foreign rule, when they refused to fall into
line; and the festival of Purim suggests a possible persecution behind its story. Most of our commemoration
days celebrate emergence from suffering of some kind.
That Josephus must needs defend his people against
Apion shows an anti-Semitic spirit almost two thousand
years old. When Rome was Pagan, it persecuted the
Jews for not being Pagan, and when it was Christian, it
persecuted them for not being Christian. Under Persian
rule they also suffered from the consequences of refusing
to conform. Even tolerant Mohammedanism swelled
their list of martyrs. The Inquisition, if all its records
were revealed, might add sad tales to the annals of our
ancestors. Expulsion from lands of their birth, the

erm

burning of their Talmuds in the market-place, the compelling them on Holy Cross Day to assemble in churches and listen to sermons that reviled their faith and expounded that of their enemies—are the commonplaces of our history. The Crusades were marked by two great incidents, the wresting of the tomb of the savior from the hands of the Turks and the plunder of the Jews of Germany. After the Reformation had set in, Catholics and Protestants occasionally forgot their animosity against the Jew, in their animosity against each other; but the breathing-spell was not for long.

After the Renaissance, when enlightenment reacted on mediæval Europe and made it less brutal, burning at the stake and torture by rack and thumb-screw went out of fashion, but the persecution of the Jew only entered another phase. He was confined to wretched quarters, called ghettos, he was shut out from all avenues of culture, from most professions and many trades; he was denied the rights of citizenship, and he had to pay heavy taxes for the right to live. The growth of more humane ideas has made even this kind of persecution impossible in Western lands. Theoretically, officially, legally, the Jew stands on an equal footing with his neighbor. In the United States, where government is completely secularized, the Jew is eligible for the highest office. But persecution has not ceased; it has only entered into a phase that cannot be reached by law. The Jew to-day is libeled and caricatured in literature, he is snubbed in society, he is shut out from social intercourse with the Gentile. Whenever we think that even this kind of persecution is over, some revolting incident is thrust before us to remind us that the old hatred rankles still.

A Christian lady, who came to me a little while ago, wishing to join the Jewish religion simply because she regarded it as the only true faith, told me of the animosity of Christians against Jews, that, with all I knew of the subject, was still to me a surprise. She told me how it was nurtured in the minds and hearts of the young, how people in all stations of life could be found who would refuse to rent homes to them, to buy goods of them, to have any relations with them, whatever, who ever spoke of them as a race outcast, abandoned, lost; that when she ventured to tell an Evangelist, who wanted to convert her, that she had decided to become a Jewess, he grasped her fiercely by the arm and told her she was about to join a class accursed of God, and that her soul would be irrevocably damned; and finally, that although her husband was an atheist, who mocked at all faiths and beliefs in general, and was thoroughly indifferent to what creed she might adopt, when he heard that she intended entering the *Jewish fold*, threatened if she did, to cast her out of his household. And so the persecution of the Jew is with us still, and because it does not take the form of violence, because we are not stoned and hooted in the streets, may be as much due to the laws of the land as to kinder feelings in the hearts of others.

Why are we persecuted to-day? When school-mistresses inform parents of Jewish children, in excessively polite and insidiously insulting notes, that they cannot admit them into their schools, when hotel proprietors append at the end of their prospectuses notices specifying the exclusion of Hebrews, or when they are blackballed in social clubs by an unwritten club law, those who are guilty of this ostracism are anxious to remind us that the religious element no longer enters into their antagonism; that they judge Jews on their merits and condemn them on their merits; that they do not wish their children to associate with them, because they are unrefined, because they are uncultivated and because they are vulgar—because, in brief, they are not conge-

nial. In looking behind these reasons, I have come to
the conclusion that religious prejudice is at the bottom
of all the others, in spite of what is said to the contrary;
that these Gentiles have inherited that religious antagonism to the Jew; that they have imbibed it with their
mother's milk; that it has come down to them as a tradition and has survived its actual cause. For that is one
of the peculiarities of prej idices—they outlast the purpose
that gives rise to them. Many of those who shut their
doors in our faces are indifferent to the question as to
whether the Jews of the first century crucified Jesus of
Nazareth or not. They may themselves be agnostics,
they may have no regard for Christianity, but they have
inherited the Christian antipathy to the Jew. The
antipathy has lasted in their natures longer than the
religion, and, as a matter of fact, the presumed vulgarity
that they object to in Jews they do not object to in Christians or to the same extent; and the bad manners of
which they accuse us are largely offensive to them because of the nationality, or race, or creed of the people
that they declare are guilty of them, as though it were
an added impertinence of this people, "rejected of men,"
to indulge in the privilege of vulgarity. And while I
do not wish to condone any lack of refinement that we
may individually or collectively be guilty of, I would
say, in the first place, that we have not the monopoly of
vulgarity, and, in the second place, that antagonism to
us has a profounder basis than that we put our knives
in our mouths or wear large diamonds.

Still I have a grave charge to bring against the modern
Jew that justifies this modern ostracism after all.
There are many amongst us who are Jews by the accident
of birth, who earned their religion by inheritance, but
do not adhere to it by conviction. They are Jews because they can't help it, because their parents, brothers

and sisters, and all their connections are Jews. They find it is their birth-right, and they accept it as one might accept an unfortunate deformity, because repining would be useless—as an added instance that the calamities of the parents are visited upon the children even to the third and fourth generation. They would endorse the words of Heine in an age that justifies it less—"It is a misfortune to be a Jew!" While they suffer the ill-treatment of the class to which they belong, they have not the satisfaction of feeling that they are martyrs to its cause. Yet they are responsible for Jewish ostracism to a greater extent than they are aware of. There is no virtue in their suffering ; they do not stand apart for an idea, because they believe in the One God as distinct from the Trinity, because they believe in individual responsibility as against vicarious atonement, because they believe in the continual progress of man as against the Fall and Original Sin, or because they believe in the infinite grace of God as against the doctrine of eternal punishment. They are not Jews on religious grounds, and those who snub *them* have a justification in saying they do not despise them on religious grounds. They are not proud of their name; they are positively ashamed of it. They are not anxious to preserve their individ-uality; they would prefer to pass as Gentiles, without, however, bearing the religious obligations of Gentiles.

It is this class who belong to us, not of their own free-will, but by force of circumstances, whose attitude partly explains our persecution now. They do us infinite harm, both without the fold and within it. In the former instance they misrepresent us to the world; they justify the Gentile in saying : "Behold a people without a religion, who stand apart for the sake of an empty name, when the idea behind that name is lost! behold a people cling-ing to a shadow, who pretend to remain distinct because of their creed long after they have ceased to accept it!" Rightly the world despises them ; they deserve to be despised. It is almost proverbial now that those who are ashamed of the name of Jew are the class that bring it into shame.

The world is right in saying they are a menace to the community, for a people without a religion are a danger to their fellow-men. The world says the Jew is vulgar; if the opprobrious epithet were confined exclusively to this class, it would be right, too. For a people without ideals, who see only the material side of life, and, therefore, work only to acquire its comforts, its luxuries, and to evade its disagreeable obligations, however faultless their external manners, however strict their acquiescence to the ceremonials of etiquette, judged by the grossness of their animal existence, are intrinsically vulgar.

I said their example is harmful *within* the fold. For there is amongst us a much larger class who stand nearer to us yet whose allegiance is somewhat wavering. Their knowledge of Judaism, as well as their belief in its doctrines, is vague and doubtful; yet they feel that they believe in this faith, certainly, if in any, for it appeals to them as the most logical and liberal of religions. There are moments when they, too, feel ashamed of their people, when they would speak of Israel apologetically; yet they realize, too, that much deeper than this passing shame is an innate reverence and pride for the name of Jew. They seem to hear a vague echo in their ears of a noble greatness behind them. Every now and then their indifference and apathy towards the faith is broken by an intuitive something that whispers of the inherent grandeur of their people, coming almost with the inspiration of a mission. And yet, in fact, the synagogue rarely sees them; they are becoming more and more estranged from their traditions. And the example and influence of the class previously mentioned, who are entirely unbelieving and entirely unsympathetic, is fatal to them. It not only makes them feel by contrast fairly observant Jews, but it is eating away the little faith left them, and is gradually undermining that Jewish sentiment, still strong in their hearts, which must always play such a large part in religious life.

The time has come that we take our stand against that extreme class who are Jews only by an unfortunate accident,—that we state to them very plainly,—if you do not believe with us, if you are ashamed of us, then leave us. To remain Jews in name, if you are not Jews in fact, injures our religious cause, encourages the negligence even of the observing, some of whom are drifting from us under the depressing influence of your attitude, falsifies our position to the outside world, makes of us a laughing stock. Your remaining with us in name and not in spirit is changing the definition of Jew and Judaism to a something less worthy. We want none of you. Sever absolutely the connections with the old name, if you have already severed your connections with the ideas for which it stands. Renounce us not only virtually but officially. Leave us alone, we who still believe in our faith, we who still believe in our mission, we who still believe ourselves to be the witnesses of God.

Why need we fear the numerical loss? Religions have never been saved by numbers, but always by minorities. This attitude of ours, anxious to claim an expert chess-player or a *premiere danseuse* in whose veins there may remain a faint trace of Jewish blood from a remote ancestor, such as is attributed to "Little Billee," has always seemed to me undignified—as though our cause were so weak that we must needs save even this remnant from the wreck. No; let us cut off the dead branches, so that all our spiritual forces may be concentrated in feeding the living boughs on the grand old tree that has nourished and sheltered myriads for many ages. Drop the Jews that are not Jews, then those that are almost Jews will be spurred on to a truer identity with the great faith.

Let us insist on standing before the world only as a religious community; let the word Jew mean that or nothing. Let us revive our old reputation—the witnesses of God, the people of God. Then Jewish ostracism and anti-Semitism will stand unmasked as religious persecution.

Never mind how few we be, if that select few be firm in their conviction, ready to stand for the great faith for which their fathers died and for which they are acknowledged the standard-bearers. Come what persecution may, we will defy it, we will glory in it. We feel that the privilege that the faith implies is worth the suffering. If our ancestors were willing to be slaughtered because of it, to meet death in the Roman amphitheatre or in the dungeons of the Inquisition, if they were willing to submit to lives of privation. quartered in dirty ghetto, and if they were to bear what has always seemed to me their hardest burden—the seeing of their children shut out from the culture and the grandeur, and the honors of the world,—surely we can bear the petty snubs to which the religious antagonism is now reduced. This is but the ghost of persecution. But, come what may, religion must not be obeyed *conditionally!* We must say—"This is our faith, for this we stand; so help us God, we can no other."

Let us not fear the sacrifices that this attitude may demand, we will school ourselves to the heroism that our position may call for; for we feel that, however, free and enlightened a country may be, however humane its institutions, however broad be the liberty it may give to all to worship God as their hearts dictate, there can be no condition of society from which sacrifice for conviction can be absolutely absent, where bravery for the cause will not at some time or other, or in some form or other, be demanded. We thank God that the age of heroism is not over, and never can be over; and that, in this epoch of free thought, when state and religion are forever separate. where physical attack is confined almost exclusively to the criminal classes of society, still denial, hardship, renunciation, contumely, persecution may often be the lot of those who stand unflinchingly by their convictions. So we will strive to stand by ours as our fathers did before us, hoping in His protection to be true to Him and to ourselves.

THE TIMES OF MOSES MAIMONIDES.

Some forty-five years before Philip Augustus, of
France, created the ignoble precedent of banishing the
Jews from his dominions *en masse;* seventeen years
before Frederick Barbarossa—"Red-beard," (how different from " Bluebeard " by the way)—or in the identical
year in which Stephen ascended the throne of England,
that is to say in the year 1135, Moses Maimonides was
born in Cordova, one of the great cities of Mohammedan
Spain.

There is a romantic, but none the less authentic, story
that explains how Jewish learning had gradually drifted
from eastern centres of Jamnia, Sura and Pumbaditha
to the western centres of Cordova, Toledo and Granada
—western then, at least.   The kindness and liberality
coupled with love of knowledge and culture for which
Mohammedan caliphs were famous, especially the
Ommeyade dynasty of Cordova, naturally attracted
many Jews.   They were more than tolerated; they were
honored and held many posts of distinction.   And since
affairs in Babylon were not very flourishing some 200
years before Maimonides was born, and they needed
funds for their schools, they sent four famous rabbis to
enlist the sympathies of their more fortunate co-religionists and induce them to lend a helping hand.   But travel
was not as simple and safe in those days as in these.
And he who trusted himself to ships was wise if he first
arranged all his affairs and said good-bye to his friends.
The boat containing these emissaries fell into the hands
of pirates and the rabbis were separated forever.   We
will follow the fortune of one Rabbi Moses; he saw that
his noble wife was to be at the mercy of these lawless
men, and both recognized their infamous intentions.

But the noble woman knew the one duty that her religion called for at this perilous moment—that she must always prefer death to dishonor. So, with the whispered assurance from her husband of immortality, she threw herself into the sea. The rabbi and his son were sold as slaves in the market place of Cordova, but the Jews made it a practice always to redeem their brethren; so they soon found themselves free. The two wanderers, walking aimlessly through the streets, poor and in rags, dropped into the college where the Talmud was being expounded. A great difficulty was reached which even the presiding officer was unable to solve. The ragged stranger rose from his seat and quietly explained the problem. Immediately the president stepped down from his chair and declared before the assembly: "This stranger in sackcloth must be your leader." And the leader he did become; for knowledge is essentially democratic and his profound learning soon made him a close friend of the reigning caliph, who, like his predecessors, was a patron of philosophy and poetry.

From the emigration of other learned rabbis, the West ceased to be dependent on the East for all its learning. It had transplanted Jewish scholarship and was going to make a name for itself. And to-day, calling America West and with better justification, have not we passed through the same ordeal? I think we have imported the last rabbi from Europe and I believe the day is not far distant when Europe will send for rabbis to America.

Moses Maimonides did not in his early years show that aptitude and energy that would prophecy the great scholar of the future. He was even said to be lazy and a dunce as a boy; strange that that should be related of the boyhood of so many of the world's best thinkers. The explanation is at hand. Boys misunderstood by their teachers are at once condemned as hopeless; now the more there is in a boy the more likely is he to be misunderstood. Tradition says that a great change came over Maimonides at the time of his brother's *Bar Mitzvah.* Hearing him praised on every side, the desire to excel was awakened. Ashamed of his own ignorance, he fled and took refuge in the synagogue, and brooding over his troubles he fell asleep and so was locked in. Awaking in the night-darkness, he felt sorely afraid. But the next morning found him a changed lad. Like Jacob, the one night alone in "the house of God" had made a permanent impression on his character. He then traveled from school to school in search of learning, returned to Cordova, surprised and delighted his father with his profound knowledge.

So much for tradition. We know positively that at about this age, he eagerly devoured every kind of knowledge that he could lay his hands upon. And, what with Hebrew and Arabic lore, his fine mind had soon a comprehensive grasp of the knowledge of the time. Of course it did not include many of the branches studied to-day. History as a study was hardly understood, for dates and exactness were considered of little consequence; what can we say of geography when the greater half of the world known to-day was undiscovered? Science in its technical sense as a knowledge of nature's laws and elements is modern, for chemistry was only born 160 years ago. Political economy had little meaning until constitutional monarchies and republics came into force. Mathematics and grammar were only partially developed. Even the Romance languages were only just in process of formation from the Latin, while much of the world's literature had yet to be written.

But Maimonides certainly made the most of what there was. He wrote a calendar at the age of twenty-three that showed much astronomical and mathematical

knowledge. He digested the whole Talmud so thoroughly that when he codified its laws he found no
necessity to refer to it. Think of that! His marvelous
memory enabled him to work without a library, and
even without the books he expounded. And his studies
were pursued under external conditions that were by no
means favorable. The reign of religious liberty was
coming to an end. Not all the Mohammedan dynasties
were tolerant to the Jews, and in the year 1145—that is,
when Maimonides was thirteen—Cordova was taken by
the Almohades, and fierce and bitter persecution began.
Ibn Tamurt wished to remove every trace of Jew and
Christian from his empire. Again it was "The Koran
or Exile." That bitter time had come when Christians
and Mohammedans were fighting for the possession of
Spain, and between the two fires the Jews had a hard
time of it. Under the iron pressure of cruel circumstances, many accepted the Mohammedan faith, as many
under the same brutal conditions accepted Russian
Christianity but yesterday. Let us not be too severe
upon them in passing judgment. Let us put ourselves
in their place! We will do much to save life. Emigration was not always possible. But to the credit of
these Spanish Jews be it said that, when exile was possible, they accepted it gladly, though it meant the giving
up of home and means and loving associations and beginning the battle of life over again in a strange land,
handicapped in a thousand different ways.

A large number accepted Mohammedanism outwardly,
while living as Jews in secret. In later days, under
Christian Spain, when the savage Inquisition made the
Mohammedan persecution almost toleration in contrast,
these secret Jews, called by their stricter and uncompromising brethren Marannos (the cursed ones), were very
numerous, and if you read Berthold Auerbach's "Spi-

noza," you will have a very fair picture of the difficulties and dangers of this double life. Now, what did the family of Maimonides do in these hard times? There was no thought for a moment of embracing the Moslem religion; but for the time being their circumstances were such that flight was impossible. There is a tradition that, pending their departure, and in order to effect it, they outwardly conformed to the ceremonies of the popular faith. On this detail the historians are not quite certain.

But, assuredly, they got out of Spain as quickly as possible, and in the year 1159 they came to Fez, in Africa, where they could openly profess the faith of their fathers. Now that his wealthy elder brother was drowned (1166), Moses became the sole support of the family, and could no longer give his time uninterruptedly to study. He took up his brother's business—a dealer in diamonds. Now, it may be asked, since he was such a profound scholar and his reputation for learning had already reached so far, and since he had begun writing many of those religious works that won him such renown, why he did not support himself in this way—as a teacher of the Jewish law, on which he had become an authority? Because he rigorously believed and rigorously practiced that rabbinical injunction, "The Law must not be used as a crown, or a spade;" that is, he would teach Judaism and its literature, and he did, but he would make no money out of it. For all the years of labor given to the compilation of his Mishneh Torah—a digest of all Talmudic law—and for all his services as rabbi, he received no remuneration. It was considered that the duties of a rabbi were too sacred for compensation.

Are you aware that this was also the ethics of the other professions—of medicine and law? Neither a barrister nor a physician could recover fees by legal proceedings against clients or patients except by contract, the idea being that the value of the services were so high that they could not be appreciated in money— the sense of gratitude was too sacred for that. This custom goes back even as far as ancient Rome. Doctor and lawyer worked not for hire, but "gratis"—that is, for nothing; hence their fee is still called a *gratuity*. We have, of course, had to give up this fine ideal for the three professions, since to-day the duties of each are so complex that they need the whole of a man's life, and would not admit of his doing anything else by which to earn his bread.

In 1165, Maimonides had to flee to Acco. Next we find him at Jerusalem, then at Alexandria, then at Cairo-Egypt; and at Fostat, the port of Cairo, he spent the rest of his life. How often our people seem to have drifted toward Egypt, in spite of its bitter associations, in our history ! Each of the Patriarchs took refuge there in times of famine ; when the last days of Jerusalem were at hand, the friends of Jeremiah fled with him there. Some centuries later, Alexandria, Egypt's new capital, became a great centre of Jewish learning—a classic period that produced the Septuagint ; and later still, one of the great rabbinical academies was in Egypt ; and here, lastly, we find Maimonides.

Here, at Cairo, Maimonides was to reach fame in another direction. He was a many-sided man, and was studying medicine. But how was a man who, through his diamond business, had wide commercial relations, who had written a condensed Talmud and also the "Guide to the Perplexed," the great philosophical work of the age, and separate treatises on every known subject of study, able to find time to master another subject, to become distinguished in this entirely new field, medicine? I suppose because then, as now, the busiest men find time to do the most things. He had the industry of genius; and a letter of his still extant, quoted later, will give an idea of a man rushed to death in a sense only understood by an American of the nineteenth century.

Whatever Maimonides did, he did thoroughly. As a physician simply, he was famous. This may be inferred from the fact that he, a Jew, was chosen one of the court physicians to the Sultan Saladin at the recommendation of his Grand Vizier—a king you will always remember from Lessing's story of the Three Rings in his "Nathan der Weise." Those were the days of the Crusades and Richard I. of England--Cœur de Leon, (the lion-hearted,) was in the East, and hearing of this great physician, asked him to become his doctor. Maimonides, not wishing to give up his present friends and patrons, declined. He was royally treated by Saladin; he had a post that enabled him to give up the diamond trade and devote his leisure to his great literary labors. But that leisure was small indeed! For his brethren sought him from all sides to answer their difficulties, ecclesiastical and social, from the resources of his Hebrew learning and his broad wisdom. He gave his medical services to the poor free of charge, and they were so numerous that he had not an hour in the day that he could call his own.

In his letter to his friend, he says: "My duties to the Sultan are very heavy and include medical attendance to his numerous household, court and attendants, which seldom leaves me free till the afternoon. Returning home to Fostat, a mile and half's journey from Cairo, I find my waiting-room thronged with patients, I beg their indulgence for a short time while I take a light meal—my only meal in twenty-four hours. I then return to my office to examine ailments and write prescriptions till nightfall.

In the evening I am so exhausted that I have to attend to the remaining visitors while lying on my back." On the Sabbath nearly every member of the congregation came to him for religious study and pretty well consumed his one day of rest. For he was really the leader of the whole Jewish community of Cairo—the voluntary rabbi and spiritual guide. Yet, he was able to write works, almost enough to fill a small library.

A consideration of these works—their contents and their influence, we must leave for a separate address. This lecture has considered only his personal life. And an eventful life it was, spent in three continents, Europe, Asia and Africa, with three distinct professions—merchant, physician and philosopher. Many comparisons have been drawn between him and the great Moses, his namesake; and in this threefold division of life we see a further likeness—for the traditional summary of the life of the Lawgiver says that he spent forty years in Egypt as a prince; forty years in Midian as a shepherd; forty years in the wilderness as a leader.

And in their vicissitudes and changes of fortune these two pillars of our faith were not unlike either; Moses, brought up as member of the royal household, soon becomes a fugitive; later we find him an uncrowned king and, next, we hear his cry: "a little more and they will stone me." And Maimonides—we find two rival kings around whom romance has thrown a halo of light suitors for his medical services, although in early life he, too, was a fugitive from Cordova. And if some of his people called him "The Light of two Worlds," there were others who called him renegade, hypocrite, even libertine. Such is the price that we must pay for greatness.

Nor was he spared from affliction in his home. His life was clouded by the loss of all his children but one, though that one became distinguished. In the year 1204

at the age of seventy he died, worn out by his vast undertakings. He was publicly mourned for three days, and
in Jerusalem a fast was declared. It is pathetic to read
that at his memorial service they chose as the Scripture
reading that story in 1. Samuel, telling that the Ark of
God was taken, and that the glory had departed from
Israel.

Here are some extracts from his last will to his son.
A will that bequeaths valuable counsel is called an ethical
will—a kind of will that is never disputed in the law-
courts:

" Serve God with *love*: fear only preventeth sin, but
love stimulateth to do good."

" Accustom yourself to good morals—for the nature of
man dependeth upon habit, and habit taketh root in
nature."

" Conduct yourself with care and with honor."

" When you ask a question or reply to one, be not
rash, speak in choice language, in a pure tongue, in a
moderate voice and strictly to the subject as one who
seeketh to learn and who searcheth for truth and not
as one who quarreleth and is eager for victory."

" Let truth by which you may apparently lose, be
more acceptable unto you than falsehood and injustice
by which you may apparently profit."

" I have found no remedy for the faltering of the heart
like the pursuit of truth and justice."

" Keep firm to your word; let not document, witnesses nor actual possession be stronger in your sight
than a verbal promise."

" Keep far from reserves, subterfuges, pretexts, sharp
practice, flaws and evasions; woe to him who buildeth
his house upon them."

" Discern the value of forbearance and you will be
holy in the eyes of your enemies."

' There is no nobility like morality and no inheritance like faithfulness."

In spite of the limitations of his time he was the greatest theologian and philosopher the Jews have produced, and one of the great philosophers of the world. And we still treasure the famous saying to which his name gave rise that "from Moses to Moses there arose none like Moses."

THE LITERARY LABORS OF MAIMONIDES.

Action is usually of more interest than thought, and, therefore, a personal life of Maimonides makes pleasanter reading than a description of his philosophy. You are all men or women, but few of you are philosophers, so while you may show but languid interest in the fine differences between the theories of the Kalam and Aristotle and as to why Maimonides chose the latter, and would hardly follow him in his flights of fancy, you would gladly follow him in his actual flights from Cordova to Fez and from Alexandria to Cairo, would feel sympathy for his persecution and sorrow for the loss of his children—rejoice in the honors paid to him by Richard I. and Saladin—devour the fables that romance likes to throw around its favorities, which tell of his early stupidity and of his later power that even controlled the miraculous.

But Maimonides holds as important a place in Judaism as Augustine or Calvin in Christianity, and since, like both these men, he stamped his individuality upon his religion, so that his influence was permanently felt, - it is perhaps our duty to know something of the nature of that literary monument he left behind him.

Before advancing upon the two great works on which his reputation is built—let us by way of skirmish, so to speak, clear the way by passing reference to other treatises, offsprings of his ample mind. At the age of twenty-three he wrote a Calendar; this implied both mathematical and astronomical knowledge, for he was an astronomer of no mean powers. In the one field of medicine alone, Draper tells us he wrote works on the following themes—medical aphorisms, hemorrhoids, poisonous antidotes, asthma, preservation of health,

bites of venomous serpents; aud an abridgment of Galen,
a Roman physican; furthermore, he was the author of
a natural history, a work on idolatry, a treatise on Christianity, a volume on logical terms.

His "Iggereth Teman," a letter to the Jews of Teman,
is one of the great letters of literature, almost as important to us in its way, perhaps, as the epistles of Paul to
the Christian. It was written to give encouragement to
his people at a time when they sorely needed it, when
Judaism seemed declining. Written in Arabic *that all
might understand it!* The Jews have changed their venacular
many times. Also a letter to the wise men of Marseilles
on astrology, warning them that it was no true science.
They could not have been very wise men if they thought
so. Indeed, his correspondence was voluminous. A
valuable addition to religion, "Shemona Perakim," was
a work on rabbinical ethics. Kiddush Hashem treated
what was a dreadfully live topic for those dreadful times,
how far a Jew must resist and how far yield when
forced to embrace another religion, in which he pointed
out the cardinal distinction between Mohammedanism
and idolatry. He wrote some poems, too, but as a poet
he did not shine. Sepher Hamitzvah, "Book of Law,"
was a preliminary to his Mishneh Torah.

And what was his Mishneh Torah? First we must speak
of a separate work—his commentary on the Mishna. It
was begun in Spain. It gives all the decisions of the
Mishna—brief and digested. Like most of his works, it
was written in Arabic, but has since been translated into
Hebrew.

And now for this Mishneh Torah—it means second
law—it really was a second Talmud and was intended
by him to take the place of the Talmud, which hope was
not fulfilled, by the way. He went through that vast
work where all the rabbinical decisions are jumbled

together and interspersed with a thousand other thing
where the discussions are long-winded and intricate
took out all the laws and codified them. It cost him ten
years of hard labor, day and night. Arabian congrega-
tions have dropped the Talmud proper, altogether, and
use only Maimonides's Mishneh Torah. Gentiles have
considered it so valuable that parts have been translated
into Latin. It was called the יד החזקה, Yad Hachazaka, "The Great Hand;" the expression "Hand of Moses"
is used often in the Bible. Now, Maimonides's first name
was Moses; יד Hebrew for hand is also the number 14,
and as his work was divided into fourteen books, grateful
posterity has called it "the Great Hand" with double
significance, and it has borne that name since. This was
the fantastic way in which works were named in ancient
times, equalled in our own days only by Ruskin. Let us
remember that the value of this book lay in the fact that
it was for the people, not for scholars. Such are the
books we want to-day, works written by scholars, but
not simply for their own small circle; we want popular
works, giving the best conclusions in lucid thought and
clear language.

It takes such a long time, as a rule, for the researches
of the scholar to filter down until they reach the people.
Some exclusive scholars look down upon the masses and
think it not worth while to write for them at all. There
is too much exclusiveness in scholarship even yet. And
he is a benefactor, indeed, who can put his researches
in simple language and simple statement, so that all who
run may read, as Huxley writes his Science Primers.

It was to serve another purpose. The logic of the
Talmud very often descends into casuistry. He felt as
mental training this might have its dangerous influence;
and since they needed the Talmud only for its laws he
would give them the laws alone. Judaism was still a

"religion of law," even to broad-minded Maimonides. This legacy has clung to us—that our creed is a code.

It was this want of a creed in Judaism that actually induced Maimonides or ר'מ'ב'ם, Rambam, as he is called by his initials, to draw up one himself, but it was by no means universally accepted and its thirteen articles were reduced by later teachers to a smaller number, Albo reducing them to three. That Judaism should be creedless to the days of Maimonides and that even then their number should be undecided gives pith to the assertion of Mendelssohn, that Judaism has no dogmas. Maimonides' creeds were formulated chiefly to answer his opponents, who sadly doubted his orthodoxy. I presume the creeds are familiar; I will only give part of Maimonides's commentary on them:—

1. The existence of God, on Whose Being all other being depends.

2. Unity of God, which oneness means allness; if one God suffices, a second God is superfluous; if one God is not sufficient, He cannot be perfect, He cannot be Deity at all.

3. God's spirituality—"not subject to motion, rest time or space."

4. God's priority—"God is the first cause, the ever-active intellect." Here we detect the influence of Aristotle.

6. When he says, I believe, that the prophets are true, do not forget his definition of prophesy is not foretelling the future—he says: "Some individuals have been endowed with such excellent qualities that their souls were susceptible of receiving the impressions of absolute intellect. In this way the highest truths are grasped intuitively." Is not this a rational definition of inspiration?

The 8th and 9th declare, that the Law will never be

changed,and that Moses is the greatest prophet, as a protest against the *new* Testament, which would abrogate the
old covenant and the new master, Jesus, who is made to
supersede the Lawgiver.

In his 10th creed, which states that God knoweth and
watcheth the secrect workings of all hearts—he really
wishes to point out the distinction between Deism and
Theism. Deism pictures the Creator as leaving the
world to itself, so to speak. Theism teaches God's per-
petual presence, providence and inspiration.

The 11th deals with rewards and punishments. "What is
the highest reward—life, hereafter; what is the highest
punishment—annihilation;" mark you, no Hell.

In the 12th creed, speaking of the coming of the Messiah,
he makes this significant remark: "We are looking forward to an age rather than to a man." This is exactly
our modern position.

In his last creed (13th), some think he intended the
resurrection, others that he implied only the immortality
of the soul. The reform Jews accept immortality—not
resurrection.

But the discussion of these problems really brings us
to the consideration of that greatest of his works, that
earned for him the titles of "The Doctor," "The Great
Sage," "The Glory of the West," "The Light of the East,"
"The second only to Moses." This work was written in
Arabic, translated into Hebrew by Ibn Tibbon, which
translation is most read by Jews, and was translated into
Latin by Buxtorf and called Doctor Perplexorum, in
which form it is most read by Christians. There is an
English translation by Dr. Friedlander, called "Guide to
the Perplexed;" there is a French translation by Munk.
Naturally it follows Mishneh Torah, to show that its
principles were based on philosophic foundation.

It is a work to reconcile the Bible with reason and

Judaism with the philosophy of Aristotle. It is a reply to doubters and sceptics; or, as we would put it in modern language, an attempt to dispose of the conflict between Religion and Science. We find that it treats of metaphysics, mysticism and the theology of Mohammedanism. Since the Moslem faith also taught belief in one spiritual God, Maimonides attempts to point out that the difference between it and his own faith is very similar to our indicating to-day the differences between Judaism and Unitarianism. Its also clears up many difficulties in Biblical language and treats incidentally of evil, providence, worship, temptation, design in nature and law; there are few things in heaven and earth unknown to Maimonides's philosophy.

Let us consider first his treatment of the Bible. It contains many expressions about God that might seem inconsistent with a Spiritual Being,—the hand of God, the image of God, the eye of God,—His anger, His pleasure, His repentance, His coming down, or going up. Maimonides reminds us that the Bible is written in the language of man, that it is hard for us to speak of God except in our human conceptions, but that we must always bear in mind that these phrases are only figures of speech.

You will be surprised to see what an advanced stand Maimonides takes on the Bible miracles. He says miracles should not be regarded as proofs of truth and that the genius of Judaism is independent of them. The fall of Adam is only an allegory to show the relation between sensation, mind and morals. The first chapter of Genesis is only allegorical. The expressions earth, waters, wind, darkness, simply refer to the four elements, earth, air, fire and water. Here we see how rational he was in spite of the limits of the science of the time. For these are the supposed four elements of

antiquity; we know of sixty-six elements to-day, and
since an element is that which cannot be further analyzed,
neither earth, air, fire nor water can come under that
category. Adam's three sons are only the three divi-
sions of man, vegetable, animal, intellectual. An angel
is that faculty of mind called imagination ! Jacob's
wrestling with the angel and the speaking of Balaam's
ass had no positive reality, they were only visions. We
must not suppose that such views passed without censure.
The Jews of Provence declared that he had reduced the
Bible statements to mere symbolism.

You can form an idea of his fine philosophic accuracy
from the fact that he scientifically demonstrates that we
cannot apply attributes to God. Only finite beings can
have qualities or relations. "When we apply attributes
to God, Power, Wisdom, Will, Love, these are only
descriptive of the works of God, implying that they
possess such properties as in the works of *man* would
appear to be the result of will, power or wisdom."
Although not a Greek scholar, he mastered the best of
Greek philosophy through the Arabic. He got his Aristotle only from a translation of a translation. The Jew
has been called a middleman in a sense of reproach. It
is true in many senses to his honor. And since in the time
of Maimonides Jews became the channels through which
Arabic philosophy reached Christendom, we may call
them the "intellectual middlemen."

As he goes deeper into philosophic abstractions using
the cosmological and ontological arguments for God, or
his attempt at reconciliation of Aristotle's doctrine of
eternity of matter with the Talmud doctrine of creation
of matter, we will not follow him. It needs a thorough
acquaintance with philosophers, ancient and modern,
with Kant and Hegel as well as Aristotle, to appreciate
these distinctions. We will also not touch his theories

about stars, planets and ensouled spheres; first, because they are too complicated, and, secondly, because they have been long ago superseded by the discoveries of modern science. Remember that in his time the sun still went round the earth, the world had yet to wait 400 years for Galileo to say of the earth, " And yet it moves." To-day you would only laugh at the idea of spheres with souls !

It was the universal ignorance of natural law that occasionally misleads Maimonides very near to mysticism,—*i. e.* the undisciplined indulgence of fancy in place of the rigid discipline of thought and investigation. The ancients fancied, the moderns experiment. But if he occasionally indulged in views about *Maaseh Merkabah* (the chariot described in Ezekiel, a popular theme for the mystic imagination), and such like cabbalistic lore, he was alive to the real problems of existence which are always the same. " For what purpose was the world created?" " In how far does Providence interfere with the natural course of events?" "Does God know and foresee man's actions?" " To what end is God's moral law revealed?" Is this really a voice of 700 years ago that we hear grappling with these problems or is it the echo of our hearts now ? He declares '' All living beings have free will, God is just and the destiny of man depends on his merits." " All religious laws are for human comfort, wisdom and happiness, for the welfare of mankind, to promote our perfection." Every law has a good purpose behind it whether we discern it or not. "God imposes nothing arbitrary. We need accept nothing opposed to our reason."

Such were by no means the prevailing opinions. His opponents said in reference to every enactment in the Law, " it is commanded, it must be obeyed, reason or no reason." While Maimonides sought rational explanations for all laws, his explanations were not always right. "The dietary laws," he says, "were only sanitary laws." And he here uses his medical knowledge to offer valuable suggestion about physical exercise. He said simple laws of health should be a part of everyone's education. He strongly condemned ascetism. Here he dealt a blow against the fasting hermits so numerous at the time. Again he tells us, "we should dress up to our means but eat below our means." His word on all things is essentially rational, he is that or nothing. "Prayers," he said, "should be simple and brief." "Sacrifice and incense were only for the primitive stage of the world" When his enemies said, "the essence of faith is blind obedience," he replied, "yes, the faith of a fool." When asked why he always looked toward the future he replied, "because my eyes are in front." But he had to answer sceptics as well as believers. We might almost think that he had to confront the doctrine of evolution when he said, "We do not remove the wonders of creation by pushing it back to the creation of an atom." He, too, realized the danger of indifference, for he preferred a sin done in innocent sincerity to a divine command fulfilled carelessly. He fought hard against formalism and superstition. As to the hereafter he ridicules the sensual heaven of the Moslem and the cruel hell of the Christian. "The future life for the good is not a garden of Eden of worldly pleasures enjoyed in idleness, with diamonds, couches and wines, nor for the bad is it a consuming fire." "He who asks what shall be my reward if I obey is still like the child who studies for a cake."

Of Christianity he says, "It has done more to spread abroad the Bible than Judaism itself; wherever it carried trade it carried the Bible, doing Jewish work with non-Jewish hands." How liberal and how true ! This remark the Gentile censor struck out of his work. Why? *They did not want it to be known how broad and tolerant Jewish teachers were.* For the same reason they struck out the famous line in the Talmud, " The righteous of all creeds shall inherit future life." The persecution of the Jew has taken many subtle forms.

But he was beyond his time. He gave to Judaism a rational and philosophic foundation which the men of his age could not understand, and which had to wait for Moses Mendelssohn who humped his back in studying Maimonides, to give to it full appreciation. They drifted back to mysticism. It was still dark ages. He had to fight against narrowness, bigotry and ignorance, and his enemies were not only Jews but also Christians. He declared that the displeasure of his opponents would not deter him from speaking the truth. Once he only escaped death by feigning death. His works were burnt in the public market places of Paris and Toulousé as dangerous; his grave was disgraced and he was excommunicated even after his death.

But the public persecution did not stop there. The authorities began burning all Hebrew books and then turned to slaughter thousands of Jews—men, women and children—they always needed so little provocation for that. But this savagery of the outside world decided the two parties among the Jews to which Maimonides teachings had given rise to become reconciled and reserve their anger for real foes. His greatness survived his degradation as with all great men misunderstood. His tomb at Tiberias became a place of pilgrimage to the very people who had once reviled him. In the public service one verse was introduced in the Kaddish, even in his life time, which read: "In your days and in our days and in the days of our teacher, Maimonides."

THE DANGERS OF LIBERTY.

It was eminently fitting that Israel should receive its liberty and its religion from the same hand, that the hero providentially selected to break the chains of Egypt should have also been chosen to promulgate the Decalogue from Sinai. The inseparable associations between faith and freedom immediately suggest themselves. When Moses appeared before Pharaoh, he based his plea for Israel's deliverance, on their desire to worship the God of their fathers. For liberty is religion's first condition. Slavery stultifies conscience, since no opportunity is given for its exercise;—there is no choice of duty, it is demanded. It is true, that, within very circumscribed limits, there is room for the play of some simple virtues. I say very circumscribed, for slaves have no means to assist others, seldom even permission; the expression of individual belief is either discouraged or prevented altogether, while there is no opportunity of regulating one's life in harmony with one's religious opinions. Furthermore, this treatment persisted in, grudually dries up the moral and emotional springs and degrades the individual to the beast of burden, for which he is used. Religion is the expansion of the soul—to expand it wants air, space, freedom.

But freedom is but an opportunity for religion, it does not assure it. Sometimes it is dangerous to religion. There is a simple, trustful faith that loves humbly to follow the leadership of others, that, thrown upon its own resources, given freedom to choose religion for itself, would grow appalled, terrified lest it might lose itself in such a boundless field, and stray off into darkness; and so it would hasten to find shelter behind stronger, braver souls who can dare to think for themselves. And even they take guidance and confidence from the authority of hallowed greatness that has stood the test of time. If the air of freedom is bracing to natures that can stand it, it may bring a chill to weaker constitutions, freezing the sustaining faith that bloomed under warm, directing nurture. The world to-day is pretty evenly divided between those who consider freedom of choice and of action benefit, and those who consider it menace to religion. We shall see that it may be both.

"Set Israel free," asks Moses of Pharaoh, "that they may serve God in the wilderness." They came to the wilderness, and—worshiped a golden calf. Freedom did not bring religion. There were no taskmasters to coerce them, they could do as they pleased, and they chose idolatry.

Emancipation has often done more harm to a religion than intolerance. The methods used to suppress the faith, strengthened it. The methods used to free it weakened it. Judaism has been as often jeopardized by its friends as by its enemies. In Alexandria, Seleucus, Ptolemy Philadelphus and Ptolemy Energetes, enlightened and tolerant, were well disposed toward Jews and Judaism and encouraged that intercourse between Hebrews and Greeks that was helpful to literature and philosophy and also broadening to religious outlook; but somewhat menacing to Israel's rigid and uncompromising morals. Another generation of it might have disintegrated our faith. If it already produced a Philo who made half the Bible symbolic, might it not have ended in the explaining away all of our cardinal doctrines as poetic symbols? As it was, this flirtation with Greek gods, somewhat idealized by philosophy, prepared the way for a Trinity and for the birth of a rival religion—Christianity—within the fold of Judaism. While Ptolemy Philopater and Antiochus Epiphanes—who did their best to suppress both Jews and Judaism—gave them a new lease of life and made possible a Judas Maccabeus and a Hasmonean house, zealous for the God of Israel. This bit of history was repeated in Spain when centuries later the seat of Jewish learning was transferred there, and the enlightened toleration of Arabic sway, while it fostered a rich, poetic literature, cultivated also a free social intercourse between Moors and Jews. This was soon followed by a laxity of observance and by indiscriminate intermarriage that might have wiped us out, had not political revolution brought the mailed hand of the Church upon us, which, trying to kill us, saved us; for persecution always begets opposition and creates heroes and martyrs. And so, in the hot fires of the Inquisition, Judaism glowed again.

When Mendelssohn emerged from the Ghetto in Germany and was warmly welcomed in all circles of brilliant learning, he commenced gladly the work of emancipating his people from the social degradation and narrow mental outlook to which the world's brutal intolerance had reduced them. But almost the first sacrifice to this emancipation were his own daughters. Their father had educated them to fit them to move in that charmed circle of literary and social distinction for which his own genius had been a sufficient passport. But when they looked at the squalor of the Ghetto, with its *juedisch deutsch* dialect, its blind formalism, its uncouth manners which almost hid its slumbering nobility and moral greatness, and then turned to the dazzling salons of the Gentiles which opened to them all avenues of refinement and culture and worldly success—the temptation was too strong. They abandoned the faith of their ancestors and joined the Christian Church. And many of their most brilliant co-religionists of that generation, for much the same reason, followed their example.

Remember, religion is distinctly a social institution;
and while it may bring together originally those who
hold the same opinions—a similar social environment
may have encouraged similar beliefs in the first instance,
and social ties will continue to foster the same religious
outlook.   For religion is more than a matter of beliefs.
It is a bond of brotherhood, a cry for sympathy—a link
binding those who stand on the same plane, live the same
life, nourish the same aspirations.   It enters our homes
and our schools, rules at the fireside, dominates in all
our family relations, regulates our joys, consoles us in
our sorrows, presides at every important event, and
idealizes and sanctifies the commonplace experiences of
every day life.   No religion could live as a cold creed
only, without the aid of the social force.   Hence the
need of the congregation—the gathering together for the
worship of God, getting inspiration from the human
multitude close around us.   Therefore, when the Jew
is emancipated, is given full political, commercial and
educational privileges, permitted to move freely in the
world of the Gentiles and to be of it, and to enjoy social
advantages from which his religion is distinct—a thing
apart—then his religious problem becomes very much
more complex.

It was so simple in the Ghetto ;   they were a social
unit there, and could, therefore, easily pervade their
lives with a completely Jewish atmosphere.   To keep
the Sabbath, to attend divine service, was to flow with
the tide.   Not to observe the ceremonial law was to
single oneself out for uncomfortable mistrust and social
ostracism.   We all move along the line of least resistance; and to fulfil the tenets of Judaism, within the
Ghetto, *was* to move on the line of least resistance.
There was no inducement to neglect the faith, there was
every inducement to observe it—that was the easier

course. Not to obey the Mosaic and rabbinical law, or
to take any new departure—that called for heroic sacrifice. Baruch Spinoza and Uriel Acosta were excommunicated, which means they were shut out from the
social circle, and the latter felt the privation and the
disgrace so keenly that he committed suicide. Under
such conditions a faith does not develop nor broaden,
but it is sure to live.

We Jews are emancipated to-day in America in the
fullest sense; we are an integral part of the nation,
sharing its duties and its rights, and at times indis-
tinguishable from the Gentiles. In the large cities there
are self-imposed Ghettos, it is true, but they are created
by poverty rather than by religion, and their ranks are
serried by many agnostic and atheistic exceptions who,
nevertheless, pass uncriticised. The religious freedom
for which we have fought for 3,000 years is ours at last.
But there are two sides to the freedom—freedom to
observe, freedom to neglect. In the Ghetto it was easier
to observe; in the world at large it is easier to neglect.
This is a Christian country in all but name; and some
judicial authorities have declared it Chris'ian in name
too; which proves, if nothing else, what an insignifi-
cantly small quantity we are, as not to be supposed to
affect the nature of the mass. The Jews are forced, by
all but law, to keep the Christian Sabbath, even though
they may keep their own too. Their children are drawn
into the participation of the Christmas festivities, by
being taught to sing the Christmas hymns, and by being
led to look forward gleefully to that time as their mid-
winter holiday, when too, the world is at its gayest;
while they cannot stay away from school during their
own festivals, without inconvenience or even sacrifice,
which often they and their parents are unwilling they
should make. And even when they do stay away, it

does not seem a holy day, for the noise and bustle of the world goes on; while there is a holy hush and all is still on the feast days of the Gentiles. They are not permitted to be ignorant of the doctrines of the Church, of its founder, its apostles or its teachings generally, for this information is presented to them in some form in every book they read and study, with occasional contemptuous reference to their own faith. They see that the Fast Days of the church influence the food markets, that the Easter regulates the fashions of the world, that Christianity marks the turning point of chronology and decides the Calendar—in brief, that they must adapt themselves largely to the institutions of another religion.

In the small town or village, where but a few scattered Jewish families live, the problem is still harder. There is no Jewish centre at all—no synagogue, no Sunday-school, no benevolent institution, not even a club. And our city Jewish clubs, by the way, without for a moment intending it, do come to Judaism's aid by encouraging social intercourse among Jews and thus lessening the chances of intermarriage with Christians. But in the country town, Judaism is maintained in the isolated families in which it is maintained at all, like some ancient, foreign tradition. The children drift toward the Christian Sunday-school, and by a social law often intermarry with the society in which they mix; though, let me say, less often than the conditions warrant. Once a year, perhaps, some impecunious patriarch is hunted up from the city and a room is engaged to hold a service, such as it is; but the young generation knows not what that strange service in that strange tongue means; they are out of touch with it; if it awakens any sentiment at all, it may be one of repulsion, forcibly reminding them that it is a voice of another age—a message not for them.

In the small places then by necessity, and in the large
cities by an encouragement that is almost a necessity,
the hold of Judaism is steadily loosening on those born
to its inheritance. The negative side of our emancipation is being eagerly seized upon, and many of our people are finding out that they can get along very well
without Judaism or any other religion, which they regard
largely in the light of an anachronism. These unat-
tached Jews are no longer put in *Cherem* as in the Ghetto
days. Whether they keep anything or nothing is nobody's
business they say; this is a free country—how such use
of "free" strikes us with a sting ! They are just as popular, just as well thought of, and even the doors of the
observant are open to them. To rebuke them would be
resented as an impertinence ; and indeed, conditions
have so changed that it is the *observant* who is likely to
apologize, finding himself the object of jocular raillery.
We have learned to be satisfied with so little that we are
glad if but the sentiments of these Hebrews by accident
of birth are at least Jewish. Any person born a Jew,
provided he has not officially renounced Judaism and
joined another creed, can be buried in a Jewish cemetery,
can receive just as many or as few rites of the synagogue
as he wishes Even intermarriage is not severely frowned
upon except perhaps by the immediate family and then
it is usually condoned. A father no longer " sits *Shiva* "
when his daughter marries a Gentile. Intermarriage is
on the increase. Perhaps there is not a family within
hearing of my voice that has not some relative out of
the faith. For, moving freely among all, can we expect
a different result ? But marriage strictly within our own
ranks is our only salvation.

By the law of association, we adapt ourselves to our
environment, and daily grow more like to it. By a principle of gravitation the large drop absorbs the smaller

drops. Can we resist the absorption, now that the Ghetto wall that separated us from the larger drop is broken down?

Such are the dangers of the emancipation for which we craved and which we have step by step attained. Do we regret it? No! For just as the world needed Judaism to supply an all-important share to its civilization, so too had Judaism to come in contact with the world's culture, with its best thought, with its most inspiring movement, with its choice souls. Only in this way does it advance with the ages and ripen with the world's growth, assimilating the highest and the best that humanity can produce. In the Ghetto, Judaism stagnated—losing its vitality and its spirit, hardening into forms from which the meaning had fled, not modifying its usages with the needs of the present, which the spirit of Judaism demands, but merely preserving—just as the insect is preserved in the amber, or an embalmed Egyptian body is preserved in a sarcophagus—ancient ceremonies and beliefs, that were probably not Jewish, but were only borrowed from antique civilization, their origin forgotten. Yet emergence from the Ghetto always brought danger. Certainly they gained by contact with many minds and new experiences, when the large world with its limitless opportunities of fame, fortune and greatness was open to them, for none so eager as the Jews, none so able as they to make the most of such advantages. But they lost too, for some, drifting too far from the fold, were sucked up in the great tide of humanity.

The Jew has always been able to survive restriction and persecution—for the Ghetto was a form of persecution : can he survive emancipation?—that is the supreme test. Can a minority move among a majority without being absorbed by it? Our distinctive characteristics are going, one by one; we are becoming more and more like our neighbors and less distinguishable from them. Some short-sighted Hebrews are foolish enough to

regard this as their ideal—thinking that, through all the
centuries, they have only been struggling to come up to
the level of their surroundings, as though we were inferior to them, and that when we are completely like them
our mission has finished.   Our struggle through the
centuries has been to keep morally *ahead* of our surroundings, to be in the van of civilization, at least in
the sphere of religious truth   Simply to become like
the nations, we need only have permitted ourselves to
have been absorbed by them—a pitiful ideal indeed.
Our sufferings would have been entirely unnecessary.
When it is your highest gratification to pass as Gentile,
then you have forgotten your traditions, and are a traitor to your name.

A minority *can* maintain its separate existence in the
midst of the majority—even as the Gulf Stream is part
and yet distinct from the vast ocean in which it is never
lost—by possessing a strong individuality, and by intensely believing in the purpose for which it stands
distinct.

In Israel's youth, when its religious purpose for the
world was only half developed, its leaders, Moses and
Samuel, saw that their preservation depended on their
standing aloof, a nation in themselves, isolated from
their surroundings; and undisturbed by the allurements
of grosser peoples, bring to fruition those sublime religious truths which were ever after to give them inspiration and stamp them before the world as a people gifted
with the genius of religion—the chosen nation of God.
In pain and struggle and much anguish of spirit, the
divine seed slowly ripened in the hearts of Israel; but
not till they emerged from the purifying fires of the
captivity, a band of zealous Puritans, were they conscious
of their divine selection.   Even later, with the gift of
national freedom came the lowering of ideals to the
elaborate formalities of a worldly priesthood.   Again
came the hand of persecution with fire and sword to
save them from themselves.   And since that day of the
dispersion among the nations, history has perpetually
repeated its experience with them.   Expanding under
emancipation, yet deprived of it as soon as too much
freedom made them forget their debts and their duties

to the past and to the future. Let us regard the wave
of persecution against us to-day, that has passed over
the world, raging fiercely in Russia, somewhat turbu-
lent in Germany and even in France, and touching us
mildly here, too, as calling us to a consciousness of our
danger, to remind us that the fires are waning, while we
have been lulled to sleep by the mild breezes of toleration. For eternal vigilance is the price of Judaism's
preservation.

We must, then, be up and doing, for the odds are
against us, in numbers, in favorable conditions, in environment. We must make up in intensity what we
lack in power and prestige. And because so many of
our own are all but traitors to our religion's cause,
therefore must the faithful few, "the remnant," be
doubly vigilant, tirelessly striving against the rising
tide of skepticism and indifference, that would renounce
the hope of Israel, even in the sight of the Promised
Land.

Because in the world at large there is so little to
remind us of Judaism and so much to remind us of
Christianity, therefore must we make our homes Jewish
homes, full of the associations of our faith, reviving the
old sentiments, so that the grand old traditions will take
deep root in youthful hearts, not easily to be torn up in
secular conflict with the world. If it is too late to take
yourselves to task—not that I think it is—see, at least,
that your children understand the vital tenets of their
faith, that they are thoroughly familiar with their own
history, so that they comprehend the meaning, the
importance, the privilege of their separation, and then,
instead of chafing against it, they will welcome it. Our
hope lies in those who will succeed us, who will take the
torch from our hand, who will inherit the mission we
have but indifferently considered. This is the age of
freedom, this is the land of freedom. Are we Jews ready
for it? Are we brave enough to walk alone? Can we
trust ourselves? Or must we go back to the confining
boundaries of an isolated nationality, to the galling
disabilities of the Ghetto, to the cramping legislation of
the Shulchan Aruch? I say again—we have survived
persecution, can we survive emancipation?

THE MESSIAH.

I am going to speak to you to-night upon an idea that at one time moved the world to its very depths and shaped the course of history. And although this doctrine is still believed in certain modified ways, it does not play the living part in the lives of those who accept it to anything like the extent that it did in the olden times. For there were periods in our history when the belief in the Messiah was a most immediate fact of life, a present emergency, a factor deciding the doings of the hour.

Although Messiah is written in English with a capital "M," the Hebrew word is but a common noun; it means "anointed," and was applied simply to the ceremony of pouring oil upon the head of the appointed king (once also it is used in reference to a priest). By this ceremony the monarch became the divinely appointed representative to the people, and almost to the present day in European monarchies the doctrine of "the divine right of kings" is vaguely maintained. "Anointed" (Messiah), then, was only a synonym for "king." In this sense it is frequently applied to Saul, David and Solomon. We find it several centuries later applied by the Second Isaiah to Cyrus, the Persian, because he discerned the hand of Providence in his benignant treatment of Israel. Here, then, we see the use of the word "Messiah" preceding the doctrine that later grew out of it. What was that doctrine? It was the belief that in time to come a man would arise from Judah who would extend the sway of Israel over all the world; all nations would become subjected to them and would accept from them the true belief and the true God. A reign of peace and purity would then follow and the world's purpose would be at last realized.

Naturally, a belief of this character did not take root while Israel was a prosperous nation under the strong sway of David and Solomon; and even in the troubled times that followed the division into two kingdoms, we cannot say that this idea as a distinct article of belief had yet been formulated, although each prophet in turn would utter some general expressions as to the glorious condition of things that would exist at the end of time, when all their wrongs would be righted and all their sins washed away. This hope, expressed by each of Israel's inspired teachers, is significant only in that it shows that our prophets took a new departure in placing the Golden Age in the future instead of in the past. It was not until after the Restoration, when Israel had established its second kingdom under tributary rule, when their political outlook was anything but bright and the religious ideals of the prophets had fallen to a priestly ceremonialism, that many of our ancestors, dissatisfied with their social and religious condition, looked forward to a time when some radical change would be brought about by the appearance of a distinct individual who would institute a new order of things. From about the time of the Maccabees this idea becomes more and more prominent in the literature of the later prophets and the Apocrypha ; and as the idea deepens into a conviction, and crystallizes into a doctrine, so it begins to assume definiteness. The distinct details of a coming time and of a coming man are now foreshadowed. The author of Daniel foresees that in process of time, some multiple of seventy, Israel as a kingdom of saints would prevail. Haggai expresses a similar hope. Zachariah is still more definite; he announces '' to Jerusalem the glad tidings that their king was coming, bringing salvation to all, a man just and lowly, riding upon an ass, and that ten men of other nations would

take hold of the skirt of him who is a Jew and say: we
will go with you, for we have heard that God is with
you," and that the great change that is brought about
by the coming of this ideal king, would be, not by might,
not by power, but by the spirit of God. As their political and social condition grew sadder, the belief in the
immediate coming of some savior to deliver them from
all their troubles grew more and more fervently intense.
Now that Judea had become absolutely a Roman pro-
vince, after the collapse of the shameful Herodean
dynasty, and was ruled with malicious persecution by
the Roman procurators till its cup of bitterness was
almost full, the one idea that tempered the suffering of
our forefathers and made it bearable, was the belief that
all these trials were but for a time, were but the darkness preceding the dawn, when God's own anointed
would appear, would overthrow the nations, place Israel
at the head of the world, proclaim God's name throughout its length and breadth, and all mankind would joyfully serve Him. As they looked back upon the past,
it seemed to them that David's reign had been the
happiest of all, that it had been really a glorious age; and,
distance lending enchantment to the view, both of his
time and of his character, David came to be idealized as
the model for their future savior, and he who would redeem them must come from David's loins. They re-read
the Scriptures, particularly the prophecies, and into these
general pictures of a better time coming in which every
prophet indulged, they read specific application to their
own days; they did not treat these representations as
poetic pictures of religious hope, but as distinct prophecies of actual events about to happen.

For instance, when they read in the second chapter of
Isaiah that "the mountain of the Lord's house should be
established above the hills and all nations should flock

to it; that nation should not lift up sword against nation, nor learn war any more," it was deliciously comforting and even inspiring to believe that this was the utterance of God's promise that would be abundantly and speedily fulfilled. When they read in his eleventh chapter that there should come forth "a stem from the root of Jesse; upon whom the spirit of the Lord would rest," for whom "righteousness should be a girdle about his loins," who would "slay the wicked by the breath of his tongue," who would institute a reign of peace, when "the lion should lie down with the lamb" and "the earth be full of the knowledge of God, as the waters cover the sea," they felt that the time was ripe for the coming of this promised servant of God, the foretold Messiah; and as the pangs deepened, so the hope was heightened. The Jewish teachers of Alexandria who imitated the sibylline style of writing, took up the Messianic cry, and the Targumim (Biblical expositions) sometimes associated it with the doctrines of Resurrection and of the Last Judgment. The rabbis began preaching it in the synagogue, and Josephus tells us that it was this firm belief that gave the impulse that decided Israel to throw down the gauntlet at the feet of Rome and to dare to wage war with the mistress of the world.

The miseries of Israel deepened and the Messiah did not come; but it is a strange law of humanity that what we intensely wish for, we finally realize in some form, and because Israel cried out so heart-longingly for the Messiah, now and then they would satisfy their own yearning by creating one. Here and there an enthusiast would appear, saying that he was chosen to lead them against Rome. There were hundreds of deluded people ready to follow each new pseudo-Messiah, for misery always encourages delusion. Sometimes the temporary success of his arms might follow, but very soon the mailed hand of Rome would fall upon the leader, regard him as guilty of treason and put him to death with Rome's recognized method of capital punishment, crucifixion.

Israel was split into sects, according to the different ways in which they accepted the Messianic belief. Of all these different parties, perhaps the Essenes were the most ideal. It was their conviction that God's anointed would realize the kingdom of heaven, that the holy spirit of God would be poured out upon the people, sin would vanish and purity prevail, and all evil spirits be exorcised from the hearts of men. Appearing at this time, showing a spirit of kindliness and tenderness to the poor in that portion of the land where the discontent was at its highest, it was not unnatural that many of the simple people should look upon Jesus of Nazareth as the long looked-for Messiah, for, indeed, they had all from time to time placed their hopes in many less worthy men; and it may be that, carried away by their enthusiasm, he, too, may have believed that he was sent as God's messenger to His people. If he had believed it—and that is one of the questions about which historians are not decided—he was certainly not the first nor the last Jew who was impressed with the belief that he was the Messiah of God. You know how the conviction in the hearts of his followers that he, indeed, was the expected savior never died out, even after his death. You know how this doctrine of the Messiah, to use the Hebrew term, or the "Christ," to use the Greek term, was continued among his followers and distinguished them as a separate sect in Judaism. You know, in later times, how, drifting further away from their brethren and accepting many of the mystical and pagan beliefs of the nations, this little sect that had begun their new departure with simply believing that the Messiah had

come and that he was Jesus of Nazareth, developed into
a new and distinct religion, Christianity. From that
point on, this faith diverged from Israel, going off from
Judaism on a tangent, as it were, to develop on distinctly new lines. Israel was now left to itself. The
last blow to its misery—and at the time it did seem to
its religious and national life—was given, when Rome
passed its plough over the ashes of the Temple and
scattered the survivors over the world.

But the belief in the coming Reedemer was not dissipated by his failure to appear in their supreme hour of
need, they still felt that it was but a postponement, that if
they would only be patient with God, salvation would
come at last. And so, buoyed up by this hope, they took
up the burdens of life again, gathering what they could
from the wreck of their lost nation nnd power, building
up their schools, teaching their children the great faith,
expounding their laws, and beginning the first steps of
their journey over the long, dark stage of Mediævalism.
But when, about sixty years after the fall of the Temple,
or about the year 130, the yoke of Rome seemed particularly oppressive, in a spirit of desperation Judah gave
birth to another Messiah. All rallied around the standard
of Bar Kochba, son of the star; and even the noble-minded
Rabbi Akiba believed in his divine destiny. From near
and far, with arms and means, Israelites came pouring
into his ranks, fully satisfied that their deliverance was
now at hand. For three years a severe war was carried
on against the eternal enemy, and there were certain
moments in the progress of that war, when it did almost
seem as though the new hero would be triumphant.
Rome became alarmed, and sent all the way to Britain
for her greatest general, Julius Severus; and then it was
that fortune changed. When the heart-broken, desparing
Israel saw this additional failure, they turned upon their

deceiver and called him Bar Kosba, son of a lie, instead of Bar Kochba, son of a star. Yet, we do not know that he was an impostor, he may have believed in himself. We are learning to revise so many opinions of rashly stigmatized impostors. Rome determined so severely to punish this revolt that Israel would never dare to repeat it, and under the savage cruelty of Hadrian, verily the iron entered their souls. Yet, they did not give up hope of a better time coming, of a savior from the house of David, springing up at some unexpected place. As the aged passed away, they would ask to be buried in the sacred earth of Jerusalem, so that they might be right on the holy spot, ready to awaken from their graves in answer to the clarion call of the Messiah.

There were some sober rabbis who, seeing that this belief was carried so far as to unsettle the people, and unfit them to adapt themselves to their conditions and make the best of them, rather discouraged it. Among them we might mention Rav Ashi. When Akiba had been looking for the Messiah one of those sturdy rabbis had bluntly said to his colleague, "The grass will grow in your teeth before the Messiah will come." But the people held on to their idea and hardly a century passed but some dreamer would turn up to be believed and followed by the multitude, a little while, till his hopes fell and he would pass away. For instance, in the year 1096, a mystic had told them a savior would appear. Alas! instead appeared the Crusaders. You know what chapter they added to our history. During the severe persecutions under the Mohammedans were many who were forced to embrace this faith outwardly to save their lives. It was but for a time they comforted themselves, the Messiah would soon come and release them. If any event particularly terrible occurred in the world, they were always ready to give it a Messianic significance.

So, when the Mongols and Tartars committed their fear-ful ravages in Jerusalem, they regarded this as the darkness before the Messianic dawn. How pathetic the picture is. Like an anxious soul long waiting for an overdue guest, starts up with a thrill of hope at each approaching sound, only to return in agony of dis-appointment, so our long-suffering ancestors saw in each unexpected incident the possible herald of the Redeemer until hope deferred made the heart sick.

In the year 1296, many of our brethren, bitterly perse-cuted in Germany, went to Syria, where they fully ex-pected the Messiah would arise. The study of the Kab-bala, the mystic science where fancies were taken for fact and pictures for realities, was particularly fruitful in Messianic speculation. Abulafia kabbalistically proved the Messiah. In the year 1295, a man from Avila gathered the people in their Atonement garments in the synagogue, to announce the immediate coming of the long looked-for savior. Moses de Leon, the real author of *Zohar*, a kabbalistic work which he attributed to Simon ben Yochai, expected the appearance of a Messiah in his own days. In 1357 his advent was looked for in Spain. A Jewish astronomer had "calculated" that the Messiah would come in 1358. 1358 come, but the Messiah did not. When Luther appeared and the Reformation took place, they gave to that great event the same monotonous interpretation; and the Kabbalists were certain the Re-deemer would come in 1527, when Rome was sacked. Many places in Jerusalem became centres of this belief, and even as late as the seventeenth century, Sabbathai Zevi stirred all his brethren in Turkey and Jerusalem by telling them that he was the long foretold redeemer come at last. Many forsook their business and changed their ways of life: but the fact that he accepted and embraced Mohammedanism and renounced Judaism, at the first cry of danger, shows that he was doubtless an adventurer and charlatan, however sincere, though deluded, the others may have been.

You hear little of the Messianic hope to-day. It is true that it is still a doctrine of Orthodox Judaism. Certainly it is the subject of Maimonides' Twelfth Creed in the words: "I believe with a perfect faith that a Messiah will come, and, though he tarry, I will patiently wait till he does come." We find the hope expressed all through the old liturgy. But it has ceased to be the living factor in the lives even of the most conservative, that it was in the olden times. When spoken of at all it is referred to with that vague indefiniteness with which we speak of the end of the world. For, living in comparative comfort, given liberty of action, our persecution over, naturally we can wait with equanimity for the coming of this redeemer. Now and then an enthusiast, even among the Gentiles, like Laurence Oliphant, will appear with some plan to colonize Jerusalem, to buy it for the Jews, so that they might return there and verify the words of Scripture. For the belief in the return to Jerusalem is associated with the belief in the coming of a descendant from the house of David who would make that the centre of his government.

I say among the orthodox, this conviction has dwindled into a shadowy belief. Among the reformers, the doctrine has been changed althogether. They look back upon the past seeing the whole growth of this idea in the perspective of history; they realize that it was a hope that grew out of the miseries of Israel, a theory that is gradually vanishing as their miseries are dying away, and that with it is disappearing, they maintain, the need for keeping alive the national status of Israel or the belief that it is to play again a political part on the stage of the word. Furthermore, while not looking forward

to the coming of any personal savior through any supernatural means, who will change the order of the universe,
they have nevertheless idealized the doctrine and expanded it into what they call the Messianic hope; that is,
they believe that in time to come, error and sin will grow
less and less, till they will almost pass away, and with the
better knowledge and the better heart that will fill the
coming man, a reign of peace and peosperity will prevail
over the earth, and all will accept the universal Father.

This hope, then, will not be fulfilled by any one soul or
by any supernatural power, but every one of us by his
individual efforts and striving after good will hasten the
good hour and add his little to the fulfilment of the
better time. We earnestly maintain that the world is
growing spiritually better, that the darkness is receding
and the "sun of righteousness arising with healing on
its wings," that we are approaching steadily nearer to
the ideals of the prophets and the realization of God's
purpose for His creatures. Not by any external force or
revolutionary change is the better day to dawn, but by
the gradual growth of the spirit of God in the hearts of
all His children, "not by might, not by power, but by
the spirit of the Lord of Hosts" will the salvation of
mankind be realized.

THE FESTIVAL OF SPRING.

Part of my text will be found in Deuteronomy, "Observe the month of Abib, and keep the Passover unto the Lord thy God, for in the month of Abib the Lord thy God brought thee forth from the land of, Egypt;" and part of it is from the Song of Songs, "For, lo, the winter is past, the rain is over, and again the flowers appear on the earth; the time of the singing of the birds has come, and the voice of the turtle is heard in our land."

Our three great festivals have a double significance. They are festivals of Nature, and at the same time have historic associations. Passover is the festival of Spring, as well as of Israel's redemption; Pentecost hails the harvest, as well as commemorates the Decalogue; and Succoth has the double signification of Feast of Booths and Feast of Ingathering.

In the festival of Pentecost, we think more of the natural than of the historical side, gaily decking the temple with flowers; though the recent introduction of Confirmation into this festival is bringing the historical side more into view. In the Passover, on the other hand, we think more of the historical commemoration, the festival of Redemption; the natural side comes only as an after-thought. And although we make a noticeable change in the service from to-day on, omitting the little prayer for the wind and the rain, which is limited to the winter service, and thereby let the first day of Passover mark the beginning of the Spring season, still the freeing of our ancestors from slavery has ever been the absorbing thought on this joyful anniversary.

I wish to-day to bring the natural side of the festival more into view, for it reminds us of our kinhip with all mankind. As far back as we can go, man has always

had a Spring festival of some kind. It was impossible
that the joyful change in the external word about him
should remain unnoticed. As the days grew warmer,
longer, brighter and more beautiful with the budding
flowers, his heart seemed to respond to these annual signs
of care and provision of the powers beyond him; he was
reminded that the harvest was soon due, which meant
food and life, that the promise of nature would be fulfilled as it had ever been, that once more she would open
her annual resources and give forth that which would
sustain the generation living on her surface.

In the Hebrew calendar a herald of the coming joy
had been already sent forth two months ago. The rabbis
noticed that just about the middle of January or the
middle of Shevat, according to the Hebrew almanac, the
first buds were beginning to appear. They felt that the
new year of nature was just dawning, and they called it
the "New Year of Trees." Perhaps you have never heard
of this obscure minor festival in our religion. It has
not been abrogated, it has simply died away. I do not
think you will find it mentioned in the modern calendars
at all, and yet it is a pretty observance with a fund of
poetry behind it. It shows that so anxious were our
ancestors to hail the joys of spring that they anticipated
it in every way, and tried to feel even in the biting cold
of January that it was at hand.

"Observe the month of Abib (green ears) and keep the
Passover unto the Lord the God." The celebration of
nature is more closely woven in our Passover festival
than you may be aware of, for even each of its historical
features has natural significance, too. There is the unleavened bread, the bread, we are told, that our ancestors
ate on the first day of their departure, when such was
the haste to depart from the land of sorrow and doom,
that they had not even time to leaven it. But we also

discover that when the fresh ears were gathered in the new harvest, the first sheaf was dedicated to God; and then *in the haste* to enjoy the new blessings of divine goodness, without waiting for the process of fermenting the people would eat the bread *unleavened*. Thus the Matzah had also a natural significance as being the first fruit of the spring—the bread of joy as well of affliction. So with the Paschal lamb, we are told that on that last day in Egypt each household slew a lamb and had it as a significant family meal, the last meal in the land of hardship—the last blow against Egyptian idolatry, says tradition. But that had its natural significance too. Just as the Matzah was the first fruit of the Spring harvest, so the Paschal lamb was the firstling of the new flock brought to the Temple as a festal offering. The sprinkling of the blood upon the door-posts, which Israel was commanded to do prior to their departure, had also its natural version, blood sprinkling being always associated with animal sacrifice. Here, then, are sacred associations connected with the unleavened bread and the Paschal lamb which you may not have heard before, that deepen their religious significance. Which came first? Was the Matzah of Passover made a feature of the Spring Festival, or was this harvest ceremonial grafted into the story of Israel's deliverance to stand as its symbolic feature? What matters? The dual meaning of this unique ceremonial gives to this festival a universality; for, be we Jews, Gentiles or heathens we all must be susceptible to the changes of nature about us. We all must in some form enter into a spring festival. Nature knows no differences between religion and religion, between man and man. When the people saunter in the fields, plucking the first fruits, and when we all go forth in the balmy air of these warm days, and feel the delicious fragrance and the stirrings of the new life, we realize that we are entering into that universal celebration, the worship of the common Father. Human differences decline, human sympathies emerge. And in that universal celebration which every people and every creed had entered in some form, we realize the kinship with our fellow-men, that we are standing before the fundamental experience of life. We are all one, subject to the same changes, the same woes, the same external experiences; we all live by nature's laws and by nature's changes, fed by its annual store; and we are all gathered in the last day to its maternal bosom. Verily one human family, with God Almighty as the father and mother of us all.

So it is no wonder that from earliest days man should have been impressed by this annual revolution. The Spring meant more light in days when artificial light was very primitive indeed. It meant more warmth in an age when people were more directly exposed to the chills of winter, and had not yet invented those wonderful appliances that are able to shut out its rigors. It meant beauty when art was not always ready to begin where nature left off. Earth puts on her fairest dress and appears before us in a coat of many colors, so that her bewitching smile is irresistible and all mankind falls in reverence before the natural miracle that has never lost its power, its charm, its marvel. When they saw the green tide come up from the south, the white snows melt into nothingness, the winter retreat like a defeated foe, and the sun, the triumphant conqueror, rise higher in the heavens, sending down its beams warmer and more direct till they pierced the frozen earth and wres'ed from its dark bosom the lovely blossoms and the nourishing wheat, they looked up to the smiling heavens, they clasped their hands, and fell upon their knees in worship.

But here it was that Israel parted company with the heathen. They both saw and enjoyed these phenomena of nature, they both were impressed by them, and they both celebrated the change in some religious way. But the heathen looked only at the physical fact; they saw fertility everywhere, and they saw fertility only, and so they worshiped Fertility; and gave to that worship gross and even obscene forms. They did not rise above nature to nature's God—the gods were nature's manifestations. Nature and her changes were the ultimate facts of the universe, with nothing beyond them, only that they believed nature was personified, that the sun shone consciously, that the sea roared with a real life, that the stars above, that the things about them, were actual personalities. Israel saw the physical universe as but the setting for the developing of the great divine purpose. They did not identify God with nature; He was above it, controlling it to His purpose. They looked not only on the natural side of life—an endless moving in a circle of rise and fall, of blossom and decay— they saw that the divine plan moves steadily on in a progressive line, that God was leading His children up toward Him, toward His own perfection. God was the personification, not of fertility, but of righteousness, and He destined His children to make righteousness their goal. Man was to see in the workings of nature but one phase of His vast purpose—must learn not always to yield to the yearnings of nature, sometimes must even suppress them. Man should look to the divine model, God, said the Hebrew prophet— must rise above nature, control it, and learn to "choose from it the good and to refuse its evil." The world within man's bosom was to be greater than the vast world outside of him; the still, small voice within, the voice of conscience, was to sound more loudly in his ears than the thunderous earthquake and more convincingly than all the siren voices of natural temptations that would gratify his every impulse—an irresponsible life, verily like the beasts that perish.

Israel brought to the world the message that man was the child of God, and because the world has tried to work out that message has it risen to the height it has attained to-day.

"Remember the month of Abib (green ears), for in that month were you redeemed from the land of Egypt." There is a charm about the spring that we do not find in the summer. The spring is the season of hope; the summer, of realization. The blessing that is to come is always sweeter than the blessing attained. The spring is the season of promise; the harvest is not yet at hand, although in the land of our fathers there was a double harvest. Our own harvest is not yet ripe; the flowers are but its prophets, telling of the plenty to come. They first peep forth their beautiful heads, to whisper of the wealth in store for us as soon as the sun grows warm enough for the treasures to be revealed. And that strange charm that steals over all of us, just when the spring is at hand, lies in the fact that it is an indefinable something that we cannot quite explain to ourselves; and because we human beings revel in mystery, we delight in the indescribable stirrings that our heart registers at the approach of spring. It is, perhaps, that we feel instinctively the good is coming, though we cannot see it. It is whispered to us from the air about us.

"The month of green ears, the flowers appearing on the earth, the coming of the singing of the birds"—these words sound like irony to some souls whom fate has placed in the lower depths of the great cities, where they cannot see the grass or hear the birds sing, where they never catch a glimpse of the country at all, but learn of it only indirectly. Some of our own brethren who are to-day singing the joyful hymns of spring, alas!

they have not seen the meadows, perhaps they will not
see them during the whole year, but, even in the hot,
muggy days of July and August, they will be shut in
their narrow streets and stifling tenements, seeing only
dirt and squalor and decay. Our poor in Ludlow Street,
in Whitechapel, in the purlieus of all the great cities of
the world, that were gathered around the Passover table
last night, that are in the synagogues this morning, what
is spring to them? I say the dearest blessing of the
spring lies in the fact that it brings to us a message of
hope. They cannot see the flowers, but they hope to see
them; their lot is hard now, but they hope that it will
be better. Those in Russia's Pale of Settlement are
uttering with very much more significance than we:
"Yes, this year we are slaves, but next year we will be
free." And perhaps those who said that verse last year
in the East feel that, under the kinder influence of
another Czar, a little something of a promise has already
been fulfilled—A very little something! And so our
brethren shut up in the Judengassen in the different
capitals of Europe, with very little of the sunshine or of
the spring verdure to gladden their hearts, yet feel the
promise of it, for nature is so all-pervasive that we can
never quite shut it out; and even in the little alleyways,
somewhere between the cracks of the stones, a little leaf
will shoot up its head and say that Spring has come,
bringing its welcome message to the homes of the great
neglected.

Spring is the season of promise. We all hope for
much, for much that we have not yet attained, that perhaps we will never attain, but yet we rejoice in the hope
of it. There is sadness now for many of us, there is
uncertainty, there is poverty, but the struggle is made
bearable and even cheerful by the thought that this will
not always be, that perhaps next year freedom will come,

There is an old rabbinical proverb: "When the tale of bricks is increased, then comes Moses." Just when Pharaoh had made the burden of slavery almost unbearable for the Israelites by demanding that they should make bricks without straw, just when their condition seemed at its darkest, the great deliverer came. We all make to ourselves a proverb of that kind. When troubles pour very thick and heavy upon our heads, we feel a change must come, and it always does. As the Spring season dawns, with its promise of better things, it tells us to wipe the tears from our faces and smile again, even though the burden of affliction, of bereavement, of pain, of sorrow, of misfortune, of loss, may have entered our homes and our lives. It tells us that verily God, the great Comforter, is at hand, and He, in His strange, mysterious way, will bring the balm to our hearts; for, behold, the dark winter has gone and the bright spring is here, the heavens are opening and the sun is shining, and the suggestion of a better time coming to all the children of men whispers its sweet consolation into the burdened, saddened heart.

I said that, religiously, man is above nature. Man is above nature in all respects. Nature makes man, says the heathen; man can make nature, says the Hebrew. What is this theory of the philosophers that climate decides our progress, temperature the nature of our government, that our art is dependent on geography, morals on heat and revolutions on earthquakes? The savage may be at the mercy of his surroundings, but civilized man learns that he is lord of creation, that he hath dominion over it and can subdue it. The message that the prophet of the Exile brought to his people, he brings to every one of us, for we know that "the grass may wither and the flower may fade, and that all of us are like the grass, yet the Word of God, the promise of

God, that will abide forever." Man is immortal, and will survive the decay of systems and the crash of worlds.

"For, lo, the winter is past, the rain is over, and again the flowers appear on the earth, the time of the singing of the birds has come, and the voice of the turtle is heard in our land." The delicious stirrings that we all feel in our bosoms at this time mean something more than the promise of the bright summer and the glorious harvest. I say again, man is above nature, and his highest and purest joys are beyond her giving. What mean these stirrings, then? Does inspiration come only to the prophet, to one man in a century? Does not inspiration come to every soul? There is no child of God but that has his fine moments, when he realizes the unworthiness of mere sordid aims when he rises to the height of his great human responsibilities, when he feels his kinship with the divine. And I think it is in the balmy season of Spring that our better nature inspires us rather than at any other time. In the Winter we must needs be active, must move fast, and put forth all our physical powers to resist its severities. In the Summer we lie down and languish, resting on the bosom of the earth. The system is prostrated ; it seeks tranquility and rest. But in the Spring, when there is just enough keenness in the air to put an edge upon our spirits, when the day is not too warm and not too cold, when physically we feel at our best—then it is that our whole system, attuned to its best pitch, affords opportunity for the higher voices within to be heard. There are dark moments when we are almost savage, when the brute in man emerges ; we get a glimpse of that in the Reign of Terror of a hundred years ago. But there are bright moments, too, that come to us just at this season of joy, when the nobility of all heroic humanity surges through us. Seize that moment of inspiration, give it immortality by making it the occasion for a worthy deed, and do not let it die away in a mere delicious ecstasy.

The Winter is over without, and Egypt is far behind, but how is it within ? Have we thrown off the shackles of sensual, material slavery, or are we still in the bondage of our passion, our unworty aims that end in self; does our gross nature still crave for the flesh-pots of Egypt, ready to renounce the promised land for its cucumbers, its melons, its leeks, its mess of pottage ? Listen to the stirrings within, for verily it is the voice of God bidding us come up higher. Each man must be his own redeemer from his self-imposed slavery; each man must be a Moses unto himself; and when God's massage comes to him to free himself, and he would answer reluctantly, like the first Moses : "Who am I ? I am not able," let him not dare to say that his passion is master and he must needs yield to its demands, and live a wretched animal thing to the last day. Let us breathe the purer air of higher freedom, that freedom to do as we should. Let us widen the distance between ourselves and Egypt, let us strive to attain to the heights of Sinai; for this is our mission, this is the whole purpose of our being here, it is why we live. Let us refuse to dwell in the valley of mediocrity, but with God as the great ideal above us, let us climb and climb, and strive and strive, grappling life's higher purposes as rungs to draw us up nearer the noblest standard. Let us not look back longingly to the stupid ease and shameful idleness down in the valley of ignoble content. Let us be up and doing.

Oh, my people, our ideals are not high enough. We are forgetting our responsibilities as the chosen people of God. The fact that we have a mission at all is almost a forgotten tradition. We are changing our character ; the old heroism of the brave Israelites has almost died out, and people tell us that the grand faith that has lived for two thousand years is perishing in the heart of the people who first brought it to the world, and whose natural inheritance it is. Let the rebuke sting us into wakefulness. The Spring season of hope is here, and surely the divine stirrings are again moving in every heart. Let us not be unmindful of the divine voice within us. Here is our opportunity come again ; "let it not go ; seize it, for it is thy life."

WHAT IS JUDAISM?

What is Judaism?—is an interrogatory that is being pressed upon us with more or less insistence. Our people are asking us to define religion for them. Is this always a healthy sign? When faith is unshaken and belief sure, there is no question as to what the religion is, it is so manifest to the inner being. Only when the spirit of doubt disquiets the heart, does the individual in a state of unrest, ask for a declaration of faith, hoping that the knowledge may lead to conviction. But belief cannot come from without. To be sure, this is better than apathy. "Tell us what to believe," asks one. We cannot tell you what to believe; there is no imperative mood in that verb. You believe what you believe, and no statement, even from the highest authority, can change it. When even given a summary of belief, we have not all religion, for there is still left out that illusive something that we call sentiment, that plays so large a part in religious life. No one can answer this question: "What is Judaism?" in a way to close all discussion and remove all doubt. You will better see why it cannot be answered as I proceed. I can, however, remove some misconceptions.

To begin with, a maxim is running the round of the synagogues that Judaism has no dogmas. Moses Mendelssohn was responsible for this statement, but we have used it more seriously than he intended and have been led to a misconception. Judaism has dogmas, as every religion must. Apart from other beliefs, the dogma of God has always been a *sine qua non* of our faith. That belief is woven into our whole history, which would have no meaning without it. We are not asked to believe it in the Bible in so many words; for ancient Israel were more than asked to *believe* in God; they were commanded

to *love* Him, as far as that lies within the control of
human will.   It *was* necessary to tell the Israelites of
Bible times not to believe in the gods of the nations.
There was a fear of polytheism, but not of atheism. Man
had not yet progressed far enough to believe in nothing,
that advance came later on.

It is true that Judaism has never endorsed the saving
power of belief as such, but it has never been led to the
illogical attitude of deed without creed.   It has always
realized that a principle must be behind an action to
give it meaning and validity.   It differs from Christianity, _
not in not possessing dogmas but in the subordinate
place it assigns to dogma.

Another misconception is that faith plays no part in
our religion.   If we were asked to explain the greatness
of our ancestors, we would say it was their profound
faith in the providence of the unseen God; that was their
inspiration.   It was that faith that made them heroes
and martyrs and sustained them in the era of darkness.
The rabbins distinctly state that Cain lacked faith and
hence committed his crime, that Abraham was saved by
faith, that faith is the origin of all good, and that its
absence leads to sin.   Here also a partial truth is hidden
in the popular error.   Faith alone has never been considered self-sufficient with us; it is a great factor for
noble living, it is not noble life in itself.   The sinner is
not always the sceptic, he does not sin on principle, or
because his opinion on authority or future consequence
differs from that of the righteous; he sins mostly because
his will is weak and his passion strong.

And now, to remove a third misconception.   Those .
who are clamoring for a definition of Judaism are some
of them answering their own question. . One, for
instance, would pin us down to the Pentateuch, and
declares that however diversely we may accept the deci-

·sions of the rabbis, he who does not accept the doctrine of the Pentateuch is by virtue—or let us say by vice—of that attitude outside the fold of Judaism.

The Pentateuch represents but one or rather some phases of our faith, and not the whole of it. Not all that is in the Pentateuch is Judaism to-day, and not all that is Judaism to-day is in the Pentateuch. It represents what we might call Mosaism. We make that same statement of Prophetic Judaism and of Talmudic Judaism. Many of the laws in these five books of Moses are dead laws, not only for Reformed Jews, but for Orthodox, too. Many of them belong to a civilization that we have outgrown; the majority of its agricultural, civil and criminal laws do not fit our time. The Pentateuch justifies polygamy, slavery, the extermination of the heathen, animal sacrifice. Even rabbinism denies much of its legislation, and dares to add to it, to subtract from it, to multiply it in accordance with the needs of its own time. It softens the *lex talionis*, "an eye for an eye," of the Pentateuch into the payment of a fine for damage. It changes the Mosaic law of the Jubilee, the reversion of land to the original owner, and the annulment of loans to enactments fitted to the more complex civilization of its own days. With less credit again, it is more lax in regard to the obligation of vows. It adds to the festivals and Mosaic dietary laws, and from a few vague hints and suggestions, evolves an elaborate system of ceremonial. Even if we would, we cannot take the Pentateuch for our guide without the Talmud. The Karaites tried to do that and sat in the dark on the Sabbath. The Pentateuch in practice involves Rabbinism, whether we would or no. To take, then, the earliest phases of Judaism and say this is the whole of it, is to shut us out of all the noble advance and spiritual progress that Israel has made since Bible times.

What is Judaism? Let us first see what was Judaism how it has grown, and what it has become. We will notice that it has passed through many epochs, that many of its earlier principles have been idealized with the vaster thought of man. How did it begin? We do not know; all beginnings are shrouded in mystery. We see the outline of the great Moses, who teaches God and the Ten Words. "Ye shall be holy, for God is holy," was perhaps the keynote of his theology. What a complete philosophy of religion and life is condensed in that great maxim—worthy, I think, of being selected by Hillel to answer the heathen, who would needs have the faith condensed into a sentence! Next we see the Prophets expanding the great God idea, imperishable inheritance from Moses, broadening that conception, until the dimensions of God were co-equal with those of the infinite universe, until His love had spread from Israel to embrace all mankind, until they realized that His divine plan was the developing of His children unto righteousness. How lightly we speak of this advance. What centuries of agony and struggle it implies. Next we meet priestism with its elaborate organization and ecclesiastical cult, embodying spiritual ideas in symbolic ceremonial, making of the fluid faith a fixed, organized religion. Then come the scribes who tried to preserve in the written word the inspired teachings of the great souls who had gone before, treasuring this word as their very life, and by this veneration for the code of precepts, representing religion as *Law* and making Israel the People of the Book.

In these later days, new doctrines come to cluster around the faith of Moses, the doctrine of the Immortal Life, outgrowing from the yearnings of the inward being, the doctrine of the Messiah, outgrowth of external conditions. Neither of these are in the Pentateuch by the way. We are in the Talmudic age next, gradually leaving antiquity for mediævalism; and yet we reach no distinct statement of the creed of Judaism. Here and there a rabbi will emphasize what he considers one or more of its cardinal teachings. Declares Mishna Sanhedrin, "He who denies resurrection and the belief in the law from heaven will not enter into future life." (This same fate is offered the Epicurean, the scoffer.)

The rabbis here and there find it necessary to make occasional statements to distinguish Judaism from the new sects and religions growing up about it. There were the Karaites within the fold, those who would accept the Law but not the tradition; there were the Christians without the fold, who accepted the Hebrew Scriptures, but after their own interpretation. So it became necessary to teach the youth what was Judaism as distinct from the different creeds about them. It never had been necessary to distinguish it from idolatry; idolatry never was a creed.

Notice, too, how late in the development of religion does the necessity for creed arise. As a similar example, grammar does not precede language, but only comes at a late stage of its development, when it is highly organized. The student of language looks back on what he found usage to be in literature and thence derives his rules. So the theologian reviews the inspired teachings of the master and deduces its doctrines from the summary. But Judaism had long passed that stage and yet it stood, waiting the codification of a creed, waiting definition. Young Christianity had already had its synods and diets, defining its beliefs with much precision and minuteness and still venerable Judaism hesitated to decide its beliefs. So it was not until the appearance of Maimonides, some seven hundred years ago, that a distinct creed of the Jewish faith was drawn up, and then

only by this individual, consisting of thirteen articles—
the number suggested by the thirteen attributes of God.
They are in brief: 1. God the Creator; 2. The unity of
God; 3. The spirituality of God; 4. His eternity; 5. He
alone must be worshiped; 6. The veracity of prophecy;
7. The pre-eminence of Moses; 8. That the Law is
Mosaic; 9. That it will never be changed; 10. God's
omniscience; 11. Rewards and punishments; 12. The
Messiah; 13. The Resurrection. Nor were these accepted
unanimously by all Jewry. On the contrary, it divided
Israel into two camps, the Maimonists and the Anti-
Maimonists. Even in these thirteen articles we notice a
local flavor, we see the emphasis of certain principles
ordered to meet the particular needs of the time. Why
does Maimonides make a separate doctrine teaching the
incorporeality of God? Because the conceptions of God
of the time were very gross indeed. Why does he specify
into two doctrines, that Moses was the greatest of the
prophets, and that the Law will never be changed? Only
because Jesus was held up by the Christian world as the
greatest of the prophets, the supplanter of the Lawgiver
so to speak, and it had been declared through his name
that a new covenant was to be given to the world in
exchange for the old, the law of Moses. So that these
doctrines are chiefly a protest. Why, on the other
hand, does he leave out the important doctrine of free-
will? Because he distinctly declares that even the
common people all accepted that as matter of course.
We miss, on the other hand, from these thirteen articles
the doctrine of the Election of Israel, which Jehudah
Halevi had so intensified.

Was this Judaism? Not all his contemporaries thought
so. And even to-day they hold but a *quasi* authority.
So far were these thirteen articles from being accepted
as a complete statement of Judaism, that one of Maimo.

nides' successors elaborates them into twenty-six articles, while the majority condense them into three. Nor are the three always the same. With Nachmonides it is creation, omniscience and providence. With Duran it is God, revelation, and rewards and punishments. With another it is creation out of nothing, revelation, and the future life. With Albo it is God, revelation and immortality. Chasdai Ibn Crescas dares to say that rewards and punishments, resurrection, and immortality are not the fundamental doctrines of Judaism, since we should serve God without hope of reward. Again Albo declares, as against the doctrine of Maimonides, that the Law of God is *not* immutable, but changes for every age. While already a teacher in the Talmud had denied the Messiah.

And yet we have no synod here, with all this elaboration. These are but the arguments of individuals, and there is no one to tell us which is the last word. There is no council or conference to draw up anything like the Westminster Confession of thirty-nine articles. So that Judaism is still left in that elastic condition, able to modify its belief in accordance with its latest convictions. The Shulchan Aruch, a codification of all Jewish law and precept, was also only the work of an individual, Joseph Karo, that gained importance from the fact that printing was invented just at this time; this helped to crystalize this work into a settled code. But it contains more dead letters for the Orthodox Jew than even the Pentateuch. To shut up a religion within certain doctrines or customs, regardless of the change and expansion of human thought, reminds us of the walls that the ancients built around the cities, forgetting that the cities would soon grow far beyond these limits, as they always did. So Judaism has grown beyond every attempt to encompass it.

It is significant that the first call of a Jewish

synod to draw up a statement of its creed really came from the outside world, and was rather a demand to explain our faith only in so far as it affected their external relations with the world at large. This famous Sanhedrin was called together by Napoleon in the year 1807, at which the rabbis declared that, in accordance with the declaration of Rabbi Gershom, polygamy had been abolished, and divorce was only sanctioned after being granted by the civil courts of the land. In the same way, it was not until the new Reform movement had been in existence some time that the rabbis of Germany thought it necessary to come together and officially declare in how far their beliefs and customs varied with those of the ancient faith. There was a conference at Braunschweig in 1844, at Frankfort in 1845, Breslau in 1846, Leipzig in 1869, Augsburg in 1871. The only changes in belief that those different conferences declared were the non-acceptance of the return of Israel to a Jewish state, the change of the doctrine of the Messiah to the doctrine of the Messianic time, and the modification of the Resurrection to a belief in Immortality. The changes in custom abolished the second day of the holidays, the Chalitza, many of the mourning customs, some superstitions, such as the wearing of amulets, the changing of the name during sickness, and the prohibition of marriage beteen Passover and Pentecost. The changes that were made in the ritual were the removal of those prayers that ask for a restoration of sacrifice, the Mussaf prayer and the Pyutim; also the introduction of the organ, the shortening of the service and the reading of some prayers in the vernacular, the removal of anthropomorphisms, the broadening of such prayers as were too exclusive, and the elimination of those that were too bitter. These reforms were not all sanctioned at one time, but represent the entire growth of the movement.

There was a conference in America at Philadelphia in 1869, and also one in Pittsburg as late as 1885, that on the whole introduced the reforms of the European conference, abolishing further the distinction between Cohanim (Aaronites) and others; and specifying the fact that Israel was no longer a nation, but a religion. Yet, all of these conferences stood rather in relation of advisory bodies to the Reform party, and none of their decisions are considered binding upon any Reform Congregation. Broadly speaking, Reform is the subordination of the ceremonial and the return to the spiritual teachings of the Prophets.

Again we stand before the question: What is Judaism? We have seen what it was in olden times, and in periods nearer to us; we see what its different denominations are to-day. Each phase has been legitimate for its time and its conditions. Whether consciously or unconsciously, the Rabbins of the past seemed to have evaded the codifying of a complete creed, while specifying practice with unequivocal precision. They thundered forth *God*, making the declaration of His unity their whole confession of faith. But at that grand monotheistic utterance they stopped, as though they need not go beyond it, all further religious growth self-developing from that eternal source. It covered at once the whole area of religion and, therefore, gave room for the liberty of personal opinion, fostered individuality of thought and sincerity of belief and allowed for religious advance in future by not hampering the coming generations with doctrinal details that the larger experience of a later day might outgrow. If we needed an object lesson illustration of the wisdom of this method, we could not have it better presented than in the present condition of the Presbyterian church. It finds itself hampered by the doctrinal conclusions of earlier times, which its best minds can no longer accept. Hesitating to reject certain creeds, sanctified by past authority, it is compelled to reject its best sons for the crimes of thoughtfulness and sincerity.

That we are not prepared to-day to give a complete definition of Judaism is not its weakness, but its strength. The profoundest things elude definition, just as the profoundest thoughts go beyond expression. There is an exquisite, mysterious something in religion that cannot be specified within sharp lines of an analysis. The conscientious Jew will not abuse the latitude here given him, any more than the limitation of an elaborately drawn up set of beliefs would save him. He cannot deceive His Maker, and ultimately religion is man's relation to God. Only let us remember, we who would give scientifically exact expression to the elements of our faith, that we are standing here on holy ground. If we only approach this vast theme with befitting sanctity, be our standpoints what they may, we cannot go very far astray. Religion is man's groping through darkness unto God. May Judaism never fall below that definition, it cannot go beyond it.

A suggestive story is told in one of Lowell's poems. An outcast fleeing from justice came to Yussouf the Good for shelter. "The tent is mine," said Yussouf, "but no more than it is God's, come in in peace." He wakened the fugitive in the morning, giving him money and his swiftest horse that he might flee from his pursuers. While harshness would only have hardened, this unlooked-for kindness completely overwhelmed him and changed his nature. A something of the grandeur of soul of his host entered the breast of the guest, and sobbing on the Sheik's hands, he burst forth: "All this thou hast done to that Ibrahim that slew thy son." Did the outraged father kill the confessed slayer? No! Thrice the amount of gold is given him to escape those who were searching for him. The black thought of revenge that had burnt in his heart day and night is gone. His son is avenged in the coals of fire that had been thus poured on the head of the guilty man. The author sums up the central idea of his poem in the words:

> "As one lamp lights another, nor grows less,
> So nobleness enkindleth nobleness."

This is only fiction, but there is a larger modicum of truth in the fiction of genius than in average history of partial chroniclers. The best fiction tells the truest facts of life in which the setting only is the creation of the author's imagination. Furthermore, we have similar instances of the reciprocal influence of generosity in the actual records of many lands. Here is one:

There are two stories told of David and Saul which vary so slightly that the critics conclude that they refer to but one incident that has come down to us in two forms. I think the double record is a further indication of authenticity. Saul had never forgotten that triumphal song of the Hebrew maidens, " Saul hath slain his thousands, David his ten thousands." From that time forth jealousy rankled in his heart, and his peace of mind was gone. David was remorselessly pursued in the palace, in the army, at the priestly settlement of Nob, over deserts and crags and mountain passes, in the wild outskirts of Palestine, to the very borders of the Philis. tines. Many hair-breadth escapes and thrilling adventures did the young warrior encounter in fleeing from the retainers of the king. But that fortune that always favors the brave never deserted him; even a cobweb was once woven between him and death.

One night he and his allies chance upon the king and his followers all locked in slumber. "There's your enemy at last," said Abishai, " let me kill him." "Destroy him not," commanded David, holding him back. Taking the king's spear, David ran up the mountain, and shouting to waken the sleeping guard, rebuked them for their negligent care of the king. Saul, overcome by this noble forbearance, burst into tears, "My son David, you are more righteous than I, you have returned good for evil, I have been foolish and wrong, but I will try to harm you no more." Nobleness had enkindled nobleness here, too.

What is the mental process of that change of feeling brought about by the unexpected and undeserved generosity? Perhaps something of this character. Here is a new view of human nature that I had never expected. I have been thinking of myself—how to revenge myself, gratify myself, serve myself—what mattered who is crushed provided I be benefited? But here is a man who thinks of me, not of himself—he is seeking my safety and I have wronged him—he gives me flight and a fortune that I may escape his own servants who are out seeking my life. Why should he do this? Or, in the other instance, I have relentlessly pursued him and twenty times tried to kill him, and have actually slain others who had defended him, and when I, the robber of his peace and the seeker of his life, am in his power he spares me and rebukes my servants for not taking better care of me. I begin to see that human nature has another, an altruistic, side that is not all striving for self, that is not so violently anxious even to obtain its just rights, it has learnt the higher blessing of giving, and the glory of renunciation. How noble this is, have I no such nobility in my nature? I am constituted as he. I will not be outdone in generosity. I despise my blindness; I am shamed into nobility. I will look in my heart for a something of that divine forgiveness and lay it at the feet of him whom I, in my depraved madness, called my enemy.

The Greek tyrant of Schiller's "Bürgschaft" who had only learnt the power to kill, saw the perfect and heroic devotion of the two friends, which so swallowed up all personal desire, all fear, all limit of sacrifice, that it did not hesitate when life itself was the test. "I see," said the humbled king, "that fidelity is no empty boast; I am conquered, you are free, admit me, I pray you, as a third in your bond of friendship." That picture of nobility had transformed him, he is a bloodthirsty tyrant no longer. You will perhaps understand a something, then, of the elevation of spirit of the Roman guards when they beheld the seraphic looks of the Jewish martyrs who were being burnt to death for the steadfastness of faith,—that they themselves were inspired with the heroism of the men they were told to burn alive, and threw themselves in the flames, seeking the privilege of dying with such heroes. At that moment they were heroes themselves, thrilled by example of their prisoners.

Each revelation of a generous nature is an encouraging reminder of the possible generosity of all humanity. When the tidings of a great heroism is brought to us, we look upon the hero not as the exception, but as stepping forward from an indefinite background of endless human greatness. It hints at the capacities of ourselves, and sends a glad thrill through us as our own hoped-for achievements loom up in our imagination. We read the biographies of famous men—Plato, Hillel, Charlemagne, Galileo, Gabirol, Montefiore, Franklin—and think what we, too, might do. We survey the great conquests in all fields of human endeavor—in experiment and invention, the brave word spoken or the brave blow struck, the toils, the struggles, the sacrifice—and feel that this is the story of a humanity that is linked to us. Cæsar stands before the statue of Alexander, and is stung into emulation. He feels that he must do something. Mendelssohn opened Maimonides' "Yad Hachazaka," and was thrilled with the determination to win a name in literature and to emancipate his people.

Alas! that the other side is true, too! We are all degraded in the degradation of one soul. Herod and Nero make us shiver, for they did what they did with hearts and minds like ours. They open up the possible depths of human infamy. We see ourselves at our worst in them.

There is a striking verse in the 18th Psalm: "The Lord recompenseth me according to my righteousness. With the pure, Thou wilt show Thyself pure; with the upright, upright; but with the perverse, perverse." Not that God is ever perverse or descends to the sins of His creatures in His dealings with them; He is upright even in His punishments of the wicked. But this is the statement of a principle of reciprocity. Good begets good; evil, evil. Sometimes we identify God with His universe and His laws. Our conception of Him varies with our character. To the savage he is cruel; to Joshua He appeared as a soldier; "to the merciful does He show Himself merciful."

We see God not only in nature, but in man. "Seeing God" means many things. It may mean beholding our ideal of achievement; and in whom is God better revealed than in a human soul—His own masterpiece? Man is created in the image of God, but he has kinship with the lowest as well as the highest. The nobility of our brother man, brings out our nobility, and his abasement develops ours.

You may not think yourselves capable of meanness; but just move among mean people, who fight for the petty vanities of first place, who hustle for public notice or newspaper commendation, who reiterate their doings in the ears of every passer-by, so that no spark of their light will be "hidden behind the bushel," who turn each penny twice before they give it forth, who raise themselves by belittling others, who pretend and flatter and make-believe; and then, even while such pettinesses aggravate you and you protest against them, you will find yourself indulging in these very tricks that you despise, if only by way of self-defense. Such small-change pettifogging humanity rouses a latent nastiness in you that you never suspected. Alas! that ignobleness should enkindle ignobleness!

If you think the world in which you live noble and good, you will be borne along on the current of its nobility. For you will want to share its best, and to be admitted, if only now and then, into the holy of holies of its sublimity. Belief in humanity, in its ultimate

unselfishness and grandeur, is one of the essentials of
your becoming morally great, too.

But if the best of men are found to stand on a principle
of "enlightened self-interest," if altruism is a delusion
and disinterestedness a lost art, where can we find inspiration to rise on the stepping-stones of our dead selves
to higher things? The exalted plane of human endeavor
that we are making our goal may not exist at all. If all
men are selfish, are liars, are immoral, then we are, too.
Why should we hope to be better than all mankind?

Hence the evil done by that cynical biography that
would steal the greatness out of every hero. When we
are told that Mahomet was an impostor, that the "mistakes of Moses" outweigh his worth, that Maimonides
was a renegade, Cromwell a pretender, Washington a
drunkard, that opportunity made Grant, that the private
lives of the men we esteem and adore would not bear
looking into, the harm reaches further than is supposed.
We are disappointed in our hopes of mankind ; we lose
confidence in ourselves, and give up the expectation of
becoming better than we are. If such are the very
greatest, what can we be? If "every man has his price,"
if "selfishness is at the base of all our motives," why
strive for a nobility that never really can be ours? Lose
but your faith in the surpassing goodness of our great
men and the latent goodness in all men, and you cut
from your feet the ground that would sustain you in
your adherence to the eternal principle of right. It is
mockery to say you believe in God if you do not believe
in men. We are not all fools, at the mercy of hypocrisy.
If a name is cherished in human annals, it is the evidence of a persistent nobility that outweighed, minor
imperfections.

It is true that good influences for good and evil for
evil, but we need not be at the mercy of every passing

influence. We must fight against the effect of inferior surroundings. A soul should not be a mere mirror to reflect whatever passes in front of it. If there is no external example of nobleness, then we must enkindle our nobleness from *within*.

I am glad to think that the bitterness dealt out to our fathers in their pilgrimage through the lands of the stranger did not quite embitter them, that if the ungracious side of their fellowmen was always presented towards them, they never quite lost their faith in the better nature that was somewhere in man, though hidden by ignorance and prejudice. And if they did not "turn their face to the smiter," nor willingly "give their coat to the robber of their cloak," they also did not nurse revenge, nor insist on their "pound of flesh," in spite of the contrary slander perpetuated in literature. They were only too ready to forget and forgive. I do not think they ever quite sank to the level of their oppressors. Ignobleness need not beget ignobleness. We *can* "touch pitch" without becoming internally "defiled."

We cannot overestimate the inspiration of goodness, but we must not wait for the inspiration to make our best effort. Perhaps, others are waiting for us to lead the way. Why should not we be the light that enkindles others instead of the dark lantern waiting to be kindled? I know of no profounder lesson in the Ethics of the Mishna than "In the place where there is no man, strive thou to show thyself a man." We must rise above the law of environment and refuse to take color from the pervading atmosphere. All humanity was corrupt, but "Noah found grace in the sight of the Lord." Humanity has advanced step by step only by isolated individuals, tearing themselves from the ranks of the commonplace, getting out of the rut of a conventional hypocrisy, fighting against the current of a debased public opinion. This is the story of all greatness, the daring to be exceptions to the rule. The man for the time raises his voice and says: "This will not do. "Not waiting to be fired by others — but, yes! getting inspiration from the absence of the elements that are supposed to create it, from the absence of all that is noble and frank, the propelling force in such instances being the vital *need* of some uplifting impulse. The necessity for better things may becoem their mother. Elijah got his inspiration to preach divinity from the prevalence of idolatry. He was goaded into his sublime appeal by a nation "halting between two opinions." Extreme ignobleness may enkindle nobleness by a process of reaction.

It was only cowardice, laziness, apathy, that a little while ago said of the flaunting iniquity of our average American politics, "What is the use? A vote for reform is a vote thrown away, the bad element is in a hopeless majority." Just because we must go around with a lantern in the daylight, like Diogenes, to find a really patriotic politician, just because the pseudo better element, hidden by a veneer of respectability and a pretense of highmindedness, is tainted with the desire to get some of the pickings, and to be in the swim with the successful organization, even though it be a muddy swim, should we be urged all the more persistently, not to participate in municipal immorality by criminal inaction.

Do not forget that, when you are dissatisfied with things as they are, with religion sunk to a hollow formalism, with patriotism reduced to a trade, with the sullen discontent of the working classes. and the heartless indifference of the wealthy, with the frauds and swindles and avaricious overreaching of what some euphemistically call "business," that you do not stand alone in your righteous indignation against the weaknesses and shortcomings that pervade all human institutions. Perhaps half of the persons concerned, even while reluctantly continuing in these failings, are, like you, dissatisfied with themselves and feel their hearts daily protest against the selfishness that makes up so much of average human life. Perhaps, even the majority are saying, "What is the use? I stand alone." And only when one has the courage to speak at last, is he surprised at the numberless responses that echo his demand. The world was never so silent as when all were to shout a cry to be heard at the moon ; for each separately refrained to hear all the others. What you think to be your individual thought is the thought of a million.

We are all waiting for somebody else to kindle our nobleness. to do our work for us, to make easy our difficulties, to shoulder our responsibilities. Let us not mistrust ourselves. A something of God's spirit is in every one of us, the noble man or woman is only the one who insists on bringing it out. The call came to Moses to bring about a glorious deliverance. "I !" said he, distrustfully, "that task is too stupendous, I am no orator, take some one else." " No," insists that divine call, "*you.*" "Go, reform your people," comes the message to Jeremiah. "I, I am only a lad." "Be not afraid, be a brazen wall in pointing out the shortcomings of your people." "Who will lead the Greeks, now the generals are killed," Xenophon asks himself, "unless a brave man puts himself at their head they will become the slaves of their enemies; there seems no one else, why not I ?"

CULTURE.

A loose use of language makes culture include civilization, education, religion, character—everything. We use grand words as a savage uses a fetich, and expect them to satisfy all our demands. Yet, culture may include all these, for we may cultivate anything, our muscle or our soul.

But like so many words that cover such an enormous area in their theoretical meaning, and that in their practical application are confined within a small range, so culture has its specific application.

It should be the ideal of every man and woman to know the best that has been thought by the best minds, to enter into the loftiest feelings that have been experienced by the noblest souls; to be enrolled in the aristocracy of mankind. We find ourselves possessed of numerous capabilities that under cultivation may develop rare powers. Our ten fingers may be trained in skill to make a thermometer, to copy nature in a picture, to draw music from a violin. Even the toes can be cultivated to do many things now done only with the hands. Every voice can be cultivated to sing at least fairly well. The memory is an elastic storehouse, that can always stretch to accommodate new facts of knowledge. Our sensibilities, like a delicate instrument, can be so finely strung as to be susceptible to every shade of emotion. Our critical faculty can be sharpened to the fineness of a hair, so that no sophistry, however faintly hinted, can escape it, but it is also able to estimate the worth of work with an exactness almost marvelous. Our moral natures are capable of great heroisms, of life enduring unselfishness, in itself evidence of our divine origin.

"Oh Lord, we are fearfully and wonderfully made." We have not even sounded the depths of our own capacities. Wherever one turns in that little world—himself, he touches some secret spring that had so far been unsuspected, and behold!—the germ of a new power. One of the many reasons why I believe in Immortality is that there is not time in one short life to develop but a fraction of ourselves. To each one, his own soul is like a vast library presented for his use: happy if he but know the arrangement of the catalogue, the names of many of the books and the substance of a few volumes, before he is called to leave it.

Alas! so many of our faculties, are like the empty rooms at the top of large mansions, unfurnished and never even explored. So many people live and die, unsuspecting their own vastness, a secret even from themselves.

There are two kinds of ignorance. There is the humble acknowledgment of one's own deficiencies and consequent deprivation, usually accompanied by reverent esteem for the wisdom of the learned. There is ignorance that is offensive by being defensive, seen in him who lacking knowledge despises it, and, being uncultured, sneers at culture, persecutes it, even tries to wipe it out. Such were the Vandals who must needs devastate every vestige of Roman art and refinement. Such was the Commune that, in its jealousy of the better classes, wantonly destroyed the Tuileries Palace, the Vendome Column and the beautiful Gobelin tapestry. To the Paris visitor, nothing is so sad as the many instances of this frenzy of barbarism. With those who have means, this offensive ignorance does not assume such violent forms. The self-sufficient solid tradesman, who calls himself self-made, is content to point to his own material success as unanswerable evidence of the uselessness of all that "book larnin' nonsense." Being beneath the world's culture, he thinks, by despising it, he is placed above it. And standing on the pedestal of material success he brutally tramples on the scholarship, dependent on his hire.

Culture is not always synonymous with religiousness and estimable character. The Puritans, grand in their sublime faith and rugged integrity were not—cultured. They explored the realms of the Right, and perhaps of the Useful, but they did not understand the mission of the Beautiful; and, in their narrowness, harshly condemned it. Art, music, the drama, were to them so many forms of evil. They did not pause even to understand them. They condemned them *a priori* without a hearing, as calumny tells us the Caliph condemned all literature outside the Koran. They were not content with being moral; they were moral fanatics; and in their zeal to *save* their souls, refused to cultivate them. They were the logical followers of the iconoclasts, the image-breakers, who shattered to pieces every statue and every work of art fearing it might be an idol.

All forms of culture, then, must be preceded by an appreciation to some slight extent of its purpose and its value. If, like the offensively ignorant, we despise knowledge or, like the bigoted Puritan, we fear art, these are likely to remain unknown worlds to us. It is a liberal education even to care for the best things;—this itself is a form of culture. He who prefers Thackeray to the Duchess, Sheridan to the startling horseplay of the modern melodrama, decoration and dress in plain subdued tints to gaudy colors, shows that he has labored and studied to cultivate his taste to this degree.

It is not easy even to understand and to really like the best things, apart from the question of creating or even possessing them. You cannot be commanded to love the best books; you must school yourselves to read them. And you ought to read them, whatever you are, professional men, business men, housewives, tradesmen, mechanics. It would be very sad if the choice literature of all languages were read and understood only by the literary few, by those only to whom such reading is part of their occupation. Yet that seems to be the tendency. You put in the plea of no time. And, yet, half the time you waste on reading rubbish, on participating in frivolous pleasures, witnessing vulgar shows, in gambling and horseracing, gossiping, if devoted to good reading—history, poetry, biography, science, essays, ·the best novels in whatever language you best understand—would make you men and women of literary culture. This warning is timely as regards ourselves. The Jew of to-day is intelligent rather than intellectual. He does not cultivate the highest kind of recreations, and people are judged by their recreations.

It has little to do with time, it has much to do with taste. We always find time for the things we care about; we seldom find time for the things we don't. To have a taste for the best and the highest implies a fine moral discipline. We must often practise self-denial to educate our appreciation. Sometimes it takes three generations to cultivate correct taste, as we are told it takes three generations to make a gentleman.

We must first learn to love all things for their own sakes and not merely for exhibiting or making use of them or because "there is money in them." In Thackeray's "Newcombes" we read of a lady, who wished to know Italian only to be heard talk Italian. All such unworthy motives are inimical to true culture. "Do not study the Law to win glory," said the Rabbins. If asked to read the best authors and the masters of style, do not ask how much money will it bring you in; but cultivate them as you would naturally wish to cultivate the best society. And the standard books are the best society in the world. An important step toward culture is to give time to things that will *not* bring in money, nor position in society either.

Learn to read certain books of the Bible simply for their literary beauty. That book has been to some their only education, to some their only teachers of style; and what an exquisite style of simplicity and strength it gives. Its phraseology is woven into our language to a greater extent than many are aware of. I have instanced the Puritans, to show that people may be moral and yet not cultured. I might also instance many scholars, who are learned, but not cultured. Learning does not always bring modesty, much as we would like to believe that it did. The reserve, the moderation, the humility of scholarship is magnificent, but it is not its invariable accompaniment. Egotistic inconsiderateness makes the scholar insufferable when he might be such a delightful companion. Johnson tyrannised with his learning, dogmatically thundering his opinions and allowing none to contradict. Some again bore us to death, with talk about their writings, their originality, their excellence, overpovering us with their learned authorities.

Genius often defies the social and moral amenities, as though natural gifts gave larger liberties, not accorded to ordinary men. We have no right to spoil our best men by dangerously encouraging this double standard. Genius has often to learn, too, to moderate its exaggerated importance of its specific gift. So many of us are defective on one side or another. There's a physician so clever and so brutal. There's a man so benevolent and so ignorant, there is a lady polished and refined, yet so narrow and so cold-hearted, that her very refinement becomes repulsive

Culture implies the harmonious development of every side of our nature, liberal education built on fine character, with the refinements of life, though cultivated to the full, still confined to their subordinate sphere.

The Rabbins advise: "Say little and do much." Do not talk about yourself and your doings, and your importance and your goodness. Cultured people do not, ladies and gentlemen do not, only conceited upstarts. Nor even let other people talk of you too much; and if pressed to speak of yourself, do so with offhand disparagement. Do not, on the other hand, assume a modest humility. Assume nothing, but *be* modest.

An unassuming manner begets a repose that is the badge of gentility, a repose that indicates power in reserve. Country folks are ushered into the presence of the great man, of whom all the world has spoken, and are dumbfounded to find him so quiet, so gentle, so simply dressed. Simplicity is the last charm of greatness and always wins.

In all these instances it will be noticed, while morals do not imply culture, what an important part character plays in culture. There is no true culture without it. Sincerity is the foundation of real scholarship, of good taste of polite manners. The genuine scholar never makes a second-hand statement, but always goes to the sources, never refers to a branch or a work with which he is but partially acquainted, without humbly and frankly confessing it, always acknowledges the aid he receives from others and righteously abhors the counterfeit and the superficial. Here, then, is thoroughness, conscientiousness, candor, honesty. A rabbinical maxim well fits this ideal: "He who makes a statement in the name of its real author, hastens the world's salvation."

And as to taste, nothing is more vulgar than fictitious refinement. It at once marks the snob, the parvenu. Be bluntly coarse rather, if that be your nature, than to smooth it over with a veneer of social polish. Artificial manners are as detestable as artificial complexions, we all prefer freckles to rouge. Be, then, genuine without the suspicion of humbug; it is the first step toward culture. Don't go into ecstacies over a fine work of art or a symphony that shows technique in the hope that you may be thought a connoisseur; but if you fail to understand its artistic excellence, patiently and humbly sit at the feet of those who know, and cultivate your powers to the appreciation of true beauty. Then you will find that the joy, the maturing of these new capacities brings, will completely overcome the vulgar desire to boast about it.

Pretension always reveals deficiencies. Those who have, need not pretend. Those who *are* important, need not assume importance. A President's valet is usually a much more imposing and pompous individual than the President himself. It is always the petty officer, "dressed in a little brief authority," who by his swelling dignity "makes the angels weep." Korah, a subordinate, wants honors and distinctions, but Moses, the leader, is "the meekest man in all Israel."

Now, a word about ourselves. Hebrews and Greeks are generally contrasted, since they stood before the world for separate ideas. Hebrews were gifted with the genius for religion, Greeks with a genius for art. The former evolved the moral law, the latter the law of beauty. The Decalogue and Venus of Milo are both lasting monuments of their respective masters. Hebrews, then, devoting themselves to the beauty of holiness, were indifferent to beauty of form. They did not religiously condemn it, as did the Puritans; they simply neglected it. This indifference certainly told in their ceremonial. As long as the symbol conveyed the idea, they cared little for its finish, its symmetry or its external charm. If the form was beautiful, it was rather by accident, or because the idea it typified was so tender and sublime—such as kindling the Sabbath lights in the home, an exceptional privilege for women; or, in the synagogue, the minister descending from the altar to greet the mourners with words of consolation. Sometimes the forms were unfortunate or even grotesque—such as the beating of the Hoshanoth twigs on the seats till all the leaves were scattered, to signify the forgiveness of sins; the sale of Mitzvoth on High Days and Holydays, the coarse details in tending the dead.

In the Middle Ages persecution drove the Jews into Ghettos, where brutal legislation did its best to make them the meanest, the lowest and the most ignorant of mankind. For centuries they were shut out of the avenues of broad education, of social culture, of worldly refinements, and were forbidden political privileges, professions, even decent trades, and were cruelly deprived of all those associations that give breeding and polish and breadth. Therefore, never a people with the æsthetic sense strongly developed, their religious forms, as well as their social manners, suffered still more under this persistent degradation. The ceremonies became in some instances almost caricatures, instead of symbols of the ideas intended to be conveyed. To those not reverently inclined they seemed ludicrous, and stirred the risibilities instead of the sensibilities. Alas! too often they were made the butt of the scoffer, both within and without the fold.

But the emancipation of the Jews and their re-admission into the world of letters and higher civilization have reacted on their religious forms, and have modified their æsthetic defects. Reform Judaism, especially of the Mendelssohn type, was nothing more than giving the refining touch so long absent. Classic music, aided by the organ, replaced the old chant. Wild shoutings and spasmodic movements in the prayers have been toned down to an orderly recital. Decorum prevails throughout the house of worship—the external semblance, at least, of reverential awe. It is an improvement in externals, but only in externals. We are beginning to find out that decorum cannot bring faith. We have no fault to find with the service in the average reform synagogue. It is simple, it is beautiful : it lacks only—believers. All these changes were right and in place ; they were mistaken only when it was supposed that they would breathe the breath of life into the heart that was religiously indifferent. Here we reach the limitations of the æsthetic. In education, in manners, we do not preach culture until the foundations of knowledge are laid. Before we preach culture in religion, refining and improving its ceremonies, we must see to it that the fundamental principles are deeply rooted in our being.

Again, in our desire to enter the world and be of it, let us not hasten to eradicate ceremonial institutions, simply to be as like as possible to our neighbors. Our individuality should be very precious to us, if we at all cherish our name and our ideals. We should jealously guard against any encroachments that assail our religious identity. The Jew who eats ham in public to show that he is "liberal" will be most despised by those Gentiles for whose admiration he is catering. Whatever may be his views on the dietary laws, there is no possible doubt about his vulgarity.

It is surely unnecessary for me to say that we can be just as cultured when Orthodox as when Reform ; that, in fact, a brave adherence to formalities that may single us out for mercantile or social ostracism is more conducive to soul culture and to staunchness of principle (that is higher than culture) than convenient negative conformity.

www.ingramcontent.com/pod-product-compliance
Lightning Source LLC
Chambersburg PA
CBHW030832270326
41928CB00007B/1013